JACK NICKLAUS

THE FULL SWING

JACK NICKLAUS

THE FULL SWING

By Jack Nicklaus
with Ken Bowden

A
GOLF
DIGEST
BOOK

Second printing
First paperback printing

Published by Golf Digest/Tennis, Inc.
A New York Times Company
5520 Park Avenue
Box 395
Trumbull, CT 06611-0395

Trade book distribution by
Simon and Schuster. A Division
of Simon & Schuster, Inc.
Rockefeller Center
1230 Avenue of the Americas
New York, New York 10020

Manufactured in the United States of America
Printing and binding by R.R. Donnelley & Sons.
Cover and book design by
Dorothy Geiser.

Photography by
Steve Szurlej and Leonard Kamsler

Illustrations by
Jim McQueen and Elmer Wexler

Library of Congress Cataloging-in-Publication Data

Nicklaus, Jack.
    Jack Nicklaus, the full swing.

    ''A Golf Digest book.''
    1. Swing (Golf)   I. Bowden, Ken.   II. Title.
III. Title: Full Swing
[GV979.S9N497 1986]   796.352'3   86-187
ISBN 0-984178-86-5 (pbk.)

To Barbara

CONTENTS

Publisher's Note
A SPECIAL SECTION FOR LEFTIES

If you're a left-handed golfer, this book offers you a rare and valuable opportunity to study a great champion from your own playing perspective.

On pages 175-203, we have re-run more than 100 of the earlier key instructional photographs "flipped" to show Jack Nicklaus as a left-hander.

We believe that constant reference to these photos will help you in better assimilating Jack's advice, and join with him in hoping this service helps you to enjoy golf even more.

Introduction

AN EASIER WAY TO SWING

An easier way to swing

I have always believed that no true enthusiast ever stops learning golf. No matter how much you know about this wonderful game, there is always more to be learned. No matter how good you become at it, you can always get better.

I have proved this to myself repeatedly during my career, but never more so than during the opening months of 1980.

Between January and May of that year, out of dire necessity, I acquired a better understanding of the full golf swing than I have possessed at any time in my career. I relearned what had made me so successful a player as a youngster, and at the same time I obtained a better mental understanding of those youthful swing qualities than I ever enjoyed at the time. Also, and most importantly, I accepted the need for, and learned how to execute, certain changes that I hoped would reverse more than 10 years of gradual deterioration in my full swing, while at the same time making the game much easier and more fun for a man in his 40s.

In this book I shall try to pass my new knowledge on to you as completely and clearly as I am able. If any of it seems contrary to what I have said in clinics or put on paper previously, then I can only repeat—with apologies, if you like—that for me, just as for you, golf is and *always will be* a continual learning process.

For anyone who may have cared to use my methods as a specific model, I should emphasize right away that most elements of my full swing remain the same. My fundamentals have not varied since boyhood, particularly not in the single, most important area of the game—the preparation for the swing. Also, the overall pattern and structure of my golf swing remain basically unchanged.

Nevertheless, I believe the changes I have made will enable me to play a lot better a lot longer than I could have with the swing I tried to use throughout the late '70s. Also, for what it's worth, I believe these changes have produced an action that is far easier for the recreational golfer to use as a model than my old one.

What caused me to go "back to school" in early 1980 at age 40?

I've told some of the story before, but I'd like to tell it more fully here because I feel it offers some useful perspectives for anyone who hopes to improve his golf through this book. The most important, of course, is that, again, if you love this great game, you never should stop trying to learn more about it.

With the help of Jack Grout, as fine a man and the best teacher I have ever known, I learned and grooved between the ages of 10 and 13 the swing I would use through the end of the '70s. It worked well for the better part of two decades and then, after a number of years of gradual decline, in 1979 it seriously foundered. By my standards I played very poorly most of that season, and I won nothing. As the year ended, I had to face the fact that it was time to either go all the way back to the drawing board or quit.

I did not want to quit. I love golf dearly, and I still wanted to play. In my heart I saw no reasons, beyond my full-swing problems, why I couldn't.

At the time it was not quite as easy a decision as that makes it sound. I was 40 years old, financially secure, very busy in business and course design, and immersed in my family. I had not worked hard

at golf outside of my own personal season—April through August—for many years. I had established an energetic but enjoyable lifestyle in my off-season in which golf was the lowest priority, mentally and emotionally as well as physically. Above all, there was the swing-change factor. I felt that I had swung the club more or less the same way many thousands of times a year for almost 30 years. Frankly, when I thought hard about that, I had some serious doubts as to whether I ever *could* learn to do it differently.

That was the downside.

On the upside were my wife Barbara's support of whatever decision I made, the growing interest and involvement of my children in golf, my physical fitness (I was probably fitter then than at any time in my life) and Jack Grout's proximity (he was wintering in Florida for the first time in many years). Also, and not least, there was my old, stubborn perfectionism, plus a feeling deep down inside that my record wasn't yet quite the one I wanted to leave behind for all those strong young comers to shoot at.

I decided to find a new and better golf swing.

For a long time, doing so was not a joyful experience, and I'll spare you a blow-by-blow account. However, as an overview of what follows in this book, I think it would be useful to describe in some detail both the technical reasons for the changes and their results.

Like all kids, the thing I wanted most when I began golf was to hit the ball as hard and as far as possible. Jack Grout encouraged this in all his pupils, first because it kept the little tykes enthusiastic, second because he believed in distance as a top competitive weapon and knew from his tour-playing days that hitting long first and then learning to hit straight is much easier than vice versa.

A big hit requires a big swing, a big, high, full arc. A big arc is most easily achieved with an upright swing. Being tall as a youngster, that was my natural inclination, and again I got plenty of encouragement from Jack. The fuller the arc, the higher a golfer will fly the ball. Grout regarded height with the long clubs as the second most important weapon, after distance, in a golfer's armory. Thus, of all the things we worked on, maximum body coiling and arm extension were always among the highest priorities.

With the distance and height factors licked, con-

trol became more and more important. By that time Ben Hogan had become a fader of the ball and was the dominant figure in golf. Grout had studied Ben's career closely and believed passionately in the high-flying, soft-landing fade as the ultimate scoring shot, especially for a long hitter. Also the Scioto course, where I grew up, submitted more easily to a left-to-right flight than to a right-to-left shot pattern. Eventually the fade became my bread-and-butter shot, further encouraging an upright swing plane.

At Scioto in those days, the rough was often long and lush, and, with my length and aggressive approach to the game, it was inevitable that I should spend a good deal of time in it. Trying to figure out a way to escape, it occurred to me that the more steeply I could deliver the club into the ball, the less grass would wrap around the clubhead and hosel and thus the farther and straighter I could bulldoze the ball from tall, wet grass. Once again, I found an upright swing the most effective way to achieve that.

Within three years of starting golf, the four elements I have just described had set my swing pattern. From then on, the plane of my full swing would be considerably more upright than almost all the great golfers whose records I would one day seek to challenge. As time passed, I remember this becoming the subject of much comment, not all of it approving, among the leading analysts of the day. Grout and I ignored the less-supportive observations, for a good reason.

Unconventionally steep as it may have looked, my backswing in those days was also exceptionally *"deep."* Keep that word in mind, because I will use it frequently in what follows. Let me explain what I mean by it.

Although my shoulders tilted considerably as the backswing progressed, which is essential to swinging on an upright plane, they also turned or coiled fully. Additionally, although my hands and arms extended well away from my body early in the backswing and climbed unusually high at its completion, they also finished well to the inside or around behind my body as I reached the top.

The net result was that I set the club not only high, or upright, but well behind my body, or deep. Looking at me then, down the line at the top of the swing with a driver or other long club, at my best you would have seen the shaft directly above or even slightly behind my right shoulder. That may not be as deep as a flatter and shorter swinger might get, but it was plenty deep enough.

It takes strength and good coordination to attain such depth with height in the golf swing, but as an all-round sports nut almost from the cradle, I was fortunate to have developed a fair degree of both those qualities in other athletic activities. Thus, although my swing may not have been the classic model of the past, with Jack Grout always on hand to help in the fine tuning it certainly got the job accomplished for a reasonable number of years.

Looking back, I believe my problems first began in 1965 when I moved from Ohio, where there is little wind, to the east coast of Florida, where there rarely *isn't* wind.

The more wind a golfer is exposed to, the harder it becomes to build or maintain a big, high *deep* golf swing (which may be why so many self-taught Texans—Ben Hogan and Lee Trevino being good examples—swing flat and fairly short). A constant wind saws at your nerves and seems to forever threaten your stability. The effect is to make you want to get the swing over with as quickly as possible. Invariably, in time, that will in some way restrict your backswing.

Also, as a youngster I was never a good wind player because I had not then learned that, to keep the ball down, the club must be delivered to it less steeply, which requires a shallower angle of attack and thus a flatter swing plane. Very frankly, it was only when I made the changes in 1980, after 30 years of golf, that I at last fully comprehended the proper "geometry" of the golf swing as it relates to the flighting of the ball.

Here I'm in my new "deeper" position at the top of my swing. Though my hands and arms are still relatively high, they are swung more around and behind my body and not as steeply upward as they were before I made this change.

Anyway, to cut a long story short, very gradually, once I was practicing and playing mostly in Florida, my backswing changed. In essence, it remained steep, but became less and less deep.

This was aggravated by the fact that, although I saw Jack Grout periodically, he was not on hand almost daily as in my early golfing years. Because you can't see yourself swing a golf club, and because feel alone is fickle, you can never know for sure whether you are actually doing what you think you are without the help of a teacher who knows your game intimately. If I had worked with Grout more often in the late '60s and early '70s, I'm sure my problems would not have become so severe. At least they would have been delayed a lot longer.

I've always believed that man mostly makes his own destiny and therefore should accept it uncomplainingly. Also, I hate excuses. Consequently, as I began to become more and more aware of this growing flaw in my golf swing, I kept it strictly to myself.

After all, I could still control the ball pretty effectively most of the time, I could still putt, I could still think my way around a golf course as well as anyone, and I had many years of top-level experience. Even by the late '70s, when I was driving shorter, playing more for the center of the fairway and hitting for the green rather than the pin, I could still win. I was not as much of a contender as in my earlier years, but I usually felt I was in there with a fairly decent chance.

That changed in 1979. It was, candidly, a struggling and extremely frustrating year on the golf course. As I have said, at the end I had to make the decision either to make the game fun again or quit.

I should emphasize here that Jack Grout, concerned friend and fine teacher that he is, did not stand silently by through my long, slow deterioration. Many people find it difficult to be bluntly frank with me, especially about golf. In his gentle, even-mannered way Jack was bluntly frank on many of the occasions we worked together. What he said, in short, was: "You have let yourself get way too upright. You are high, which is good, but you have lost your depth, which is very bad. If you don't do something about that, your career will be a lot shorter than either of us would like it to be."

The problem was that I heard Jack, but didn't really listen. Periodically we would work a little on deepening my swing, but there was no way I could

make it happen quickly and reliably. Fearful of falling between a new method and an old one, fearful of losing whatever I did have left, I simply wasn't ready to make the commitment in time and effort necessary, in effect, to learn a new golf swing.

When the commitment finally was made at the beginning of 1980, the initial changes were not made on the practice tee. First, with the willing cooperation of my business associates within and without Golden Bear, Inc., I reduced my nongolf activities to an absolute minimum, at least through the Masters. Second, I made it a rule that instead of going to the office in the morning and the golf course, maybe, in the afternoon, I would definitely go to the golf course in the morning and the office, maybe, in the afternoon. Third, I persuaded Jack Grout not only to reside for some months within about a drive and 3-wood of my home, but to be on hand every day, as he was, so helpfully, during my early years.

To understand the changes we set about trying to make, you have to understand the type of impact created by an overupright swing plane, plus the effect on clubhead speed of not swinging deep enough going back.

The more upright the swing, the more downward or less level the arc of the clubhead through impact. The steeper or more downward the clubhead arc, the tougher it becomes to hit the ball squarely in the meat. Instead, you get what I call, from its feel, an "oblique" kind of hit—a sense of always catching the ball with a slightly glancing blow, rather than that lovely sensation when you sock it solidly in the rear. I had become very familiar with bad-feeling golf shots during the late '70s.

Distance in golf is the product of clubhead speed squarely applied. One of the lessons I relearned in early 1980 is that squareness depends just as much on the angle of the club's approach to the ball as it does on the path of the club relative to the target line. I was losing some distance, plus some degree of flight control, by delivering the club to the ball too steeply—by hitting it too obliquely. However, this same steepness was also causing me to lose even more distance by decreasing my clubhead speed.

Clubhead speed in the golf swing ultimately is the product of centrifugal force, which in turn is largely created by torsion or leverage. To oversimplify a little for the sake of clarity, the *deeper* your backswing, the more torsion or leverage you are able to generate to release in the form of centrifugal force on the through-swing. To put this another way, the less you *turn* your upper body and swing your arms and hands *behind* your upper body going back, the less clubhead speed you generate and the shorter you hit the ball.

The degree to which a golfer coils his body going back is heavily influenced by his arm swing. The more directly upward rather than *upward and rearward* the arms are swung, the sooner the body will stop coiling. This is an involuntary reaction caused by the false sense of having made a complete backswing created by high-swinging arms. It's a lazy, lift-up-and-chop way to play, extremely common among recreational golfers and maybe the single biggest reason they hit the ball so lifelessly and so short.

''Complete the backswing'' has been my No. One key thought all through my career, but I found it progressively more difficult during the late '70s to attain the old sense of being fully ''wound'' at the top. As I have said, I had begun to hit the ball noticeably shorter. The problem lay in too steep an angle of attack as the result of an insufficiently deep backswing.

The challenge, then, as Grout and I began work at the beginning of 1980, was in essence simply to deepen or flatten my swing sufficiently to produce a shallower or less-acute clubhead arc through impact.

Sounds simple? Well, if you've ever had a long-standing golfing fault and have made a 1,000 percent emotional commitment to cure it, and then have actually put yourself to work, I don't have to spell out how incredibly difficult it can be to make so seemingly small a change. No matter how strong the will, the flesh can be amazingly stubborn. Time and again I would think I had it, only to watch Grout and others who were on hand and who know my game somberly shake their heads. It was *tough*.

Essentially, I was to make three swing changes over a period of about four months. Each was integral to the others, so I had little option but to work on them simultaneouly. For the sake of clarity, however, I had better try to describe each separately.

These pictures show the change in my address position from old (above) to new (right). Now my upper body is more erect, which makes my head and shoulders taller, a situation I try to maintain throughout the swing.

Change No. 1
Stand taller at address

The first and probably the most critical change I had to master was to stand taller to the ball at address and then stay tall—maintain my height in the hips, shoulders and head—throughout the swing.

The more inclined the body at address, the more the shoulders and hips will tend to tilt and the head to dip during the backswing. The greater these tilts and dips, the harder it is to genuinely turn the upper body and arms away from the ball and behind yourself, and thus the more upright the swing plane will be.

Even in the good old days I had to watch a tendency to get too inclined or "over" the ball at address, chiefly by letting my head drop too low. Now, set up as tall as Grout wanted me, I felt at first like a soldier on parade—virtually standing at attention. Worse was the feeling that, even if I made a decent backswing from such an uncomfortable posture, I would never get the clubhead back to the ball before I swung around and over with my shoulders. In short, I felt just like I imagine many golfers who slice all their shots feel most of the time.

With admirable patience, Grout eventually convinced me that the cause of this feeling was restricted clubhead release born of the over-upright, over-tilted backswing. Being too "low" with my upper body during the swing, I had developed an involuntary restraint with the hands and wrists to avoid hitting behind the ball and/or from out to in across the ball. Jack summed it up well when he explained that I hadn't experienced full extension at the ball in years, and that a golfer cannot achieve full clubhead release without achieving full extension at the ball.

Sessions like this explained my inability to hit controlled low shots, my hefty divots with medium and short irons, and the sharply inward path of my divots immediately after impact. When eventually I did learn to stand up and stay up, then let everything fly early enough to achieve full extension at impact, I found I got the clubhead to the ball just fine before my shoulders swung out and over. Also, my divots became shallower and straighter, I could hit low shots with far less strain, and, most encouraging of all, much of my old distance began to return.

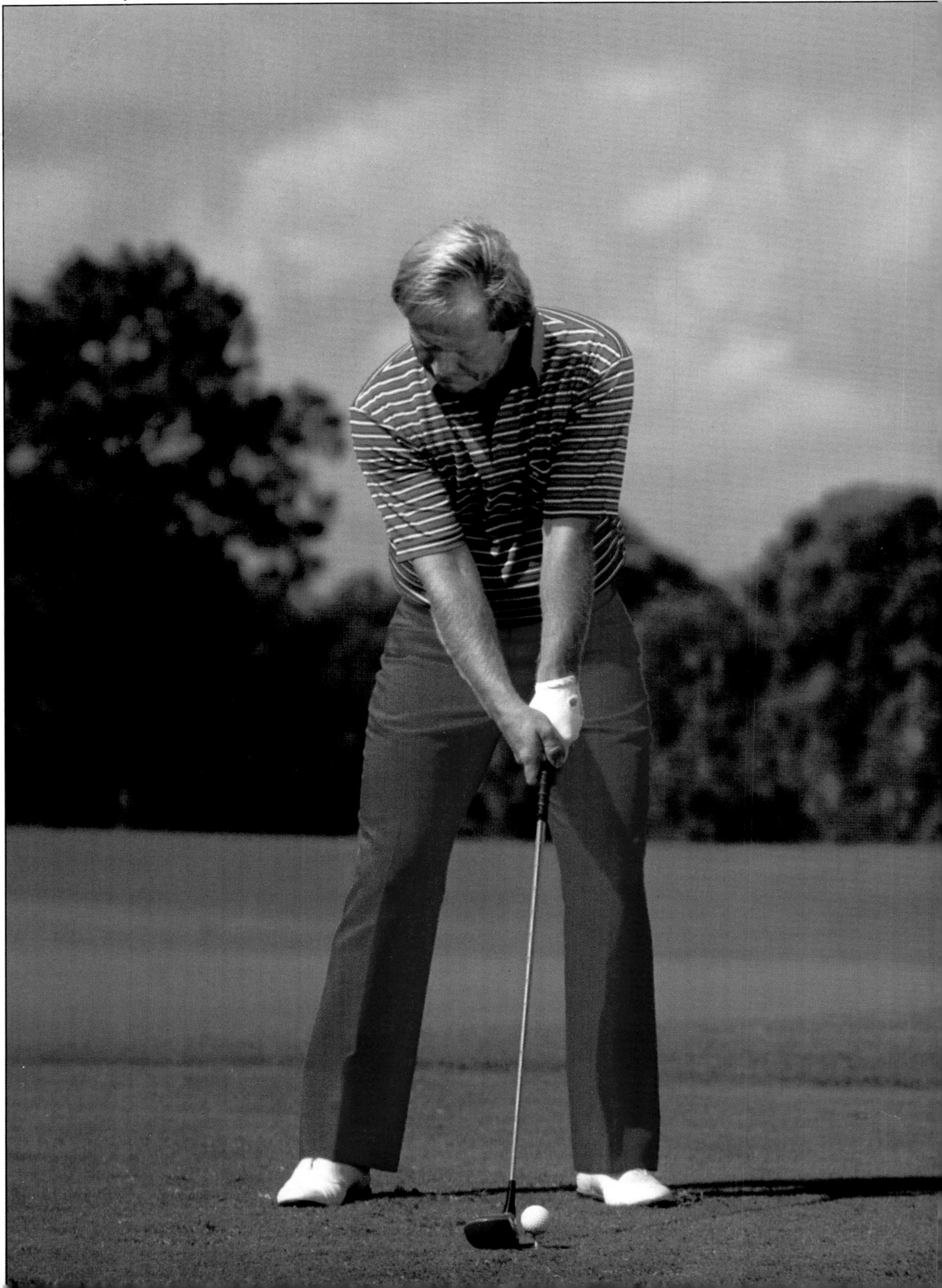

Change No. 2
Head more centered

My second important change involved head and ball positioning at address.

The more upright the swing, the more the legs must drive forward coming down and through to keep the clubhead from passing beyond the target line before impact. The more leg-drive a golfer uses, the farther back he feels he must set his head to insure against it shifting forward with the lower-body motion. Also, he must position the ball well forward to insure that he catches it cleanly at the bottom of the swing arc.

My legs were always by far the strongest parts of my body, and as a youngster that suited me just fine. Time, however, does indeed take its toll. As I had got older, it had become more and more difficult to work my legs as forcefully as a very upright swing demanded, and the more so the less deeply I swung.

Then we come to the somewhat subtle manner of the effect of head position on the shape of the backswing.

The best way I can explain this is to ask you to conduct a little experiment. Take one of your longer clubs and set up with your head where the good Lord put it—more or less centered over your body. Now begin the backswing by turning your shoulders and arms, working as a unit, *directly* away from the ball. You will have made the move correctly if both your upper arms stay close to your chest and the club swings quickly to the inside of the target line. When you do it correctly, you should find it a natural and easy turning motion with very little tilting of the shoulders.

Now set up again, but this time move your head backward or away from the target so that it is positioned more or less over your right leg. Now try to turn directly away from the ball as you did before. At best, I think you will find this difficult to do. At worst, you will find your arms swinging outward and upward away from your body, while your shoulders tilt at least as much as they turn.

For almost my entire career I played with my head set well back at address, which pre-established wide-extending, high-swinging arms and a large degree of tilt in my shoulder action. When

Whereas before, I used to set up with my head back, almost over my right leg (above), now my head is more centered, set just behind the ball (left). With my new head position, I can more easily turn my upper body and swing my arms inward and upward.

Jack finally persuaded me to center my head and leave it there, it immediately became a great deal easier to genuinely *turn* my upper body and swing my arms *inward* and upward from the moment the club left the ball.

All I regret now is that I took so darn much persuading, because this change in head position truly was a landmark in the relearning process. Combined with the more-erect posture, the new head position began to produce a definite—and, most importantly, *repeatable*—deepening or flattening of my backswing.

However, the flatter the backswing becomes, the less downswing leg-drive is needed. I now found the club was reaching the bottom of its arc slightly behind its previous low point. The solution to that was the easiest of all the changes I would finally make: I simply moved the ball a little farther back in my stance.

Instead of my right elbow "flying" as it did so famously for 30 years (above), it now folds more quickly and remains closer to my side going back. This lets the club swing inside sooner and promotes that deeper backswing.

Change No. 3
Right elbow folds earlier

The third and last of my major changes, involving the arm swing, represents the biggest departure from my previous methods.

Until 1980 it was difficult for me to imagine any good golfer playing his best with less than the widest possible clubhead arc on both sides of the ball. For that reason, I had always placed heavy stress on maximum arm extension, both in my own game and in my clinics and writings. I strongly believed and frequently wrote that the farther the arms swing away from the body going back the better, the same being true on the follow-through.

If a golfer can swing his arms as deeply behind him while fully extending them away from his body as I could 20 years ago, that may still be good advice, because there is no question that the biggest *deep* arc produces the biggest golf shots. The problems occur when the depth diminishes.

As I now know from painful experience, if the arms are overly extended early in the backswing they will generally move outward and upward both too quickly and too far, relative to the turning of the upper body. By promoting a false sense of a completed backswing, this cuts short the body coiling that would help produce the needed depth.

I finally escaped this vicious circle by virtually reversing my concept of the proper arm swing.

Instead of extending my arms directly back from the ball and separating them from my torso as much as possible, I began hugging the upper parts to my chest, at least during the first half of the backswing. To achieve this, I found I had to allow the right elbow—you know, the one that "flew" for 30 years—to fold or break as soon as the club started back, then keep it as close to my right side as I could for as long as I could. To facilitate both these moves, I found I needed to weaken my grip slightly, by turning my hands a little more to the left. Also, I mentally had to condition myself to seeing the clubhead in my peripheral vision swing far more quickly inside the target line, with the face appearing to open much faster than ever before.

Four views of my new swing

Finally, with the club at last properly positioned at the top, I had to discipline myself to achieve complete extension at impact by releasing fully the moment I had moved to my left side starting down—to really sling the clubhead into the ball with my hands and wrists as fast and freely as I possibly could. Maximum release from the top of the backswing had been a lifelong fundamental for me, but with a swing fault such as I've described it had become impossible to apply. What a joy it was by the spring of 1980 to be able to really whap that ball solidly in the rear again!

With the exception of a full release, for almost 30 years I would have regarded all of the above moves as raging heresy. In combination, they proved to be the final keys to resurrecting my golf swing.

By standing taller and shifting my head and the ball, I had put myself in a new position that made swinging the club *behind* me, as well as up above me, a great deal easier. By letting my arms swing *in* and up rather than *out* and up, I finally got the club into a position from which I could repeatedly and reflexively release it fully into the ball along the proper path and at the proper angle and at the proper speed.

Those were my three biggest changes. There have been some other refinements, partly in support of the three main ones and partly as a result of them. I'll describe those as we get to the appropriate sections of the swing.

I would like to conclude this overview of a mid-life learning experience by summarizing what it has done for my game.

First, I regained a great deal of lost distance—I'm not as long as I was at 21, but I'm not bad for double that age. Second, I regained an almost-lost ability to hit controlled right-to-left shots—so much so that I now intentionally draw the ball with the longer clubs more often than I fade it. Third, all my iron shots became much crisper—with a particularly dramatic improvement in the short irons, my lifelong weakness. Fourth, I found a physically easier way to swing a golf club just at a point in life where I really needed one—I still use a lot of body action, but am now far more of a "hands player" than I ever believed I would be. Fifth, I regained total confidence in my ability to compete for a few more years. Sixth, and by far the most important, golf became fun again.

I hope this book will help you to keep on enjoying golf for a long time, too.

Part One
PREPARING TO SWING

Chapter 1

Holding the club

Your grip is the foundation of your swing

Early each January now for many years, with the holidays over and family life getting back to normal and another Masters clearly on the horizon, I have got the golf bug. Usually I will have played very little for three or four months, which intensifies the itch. More often than not, memories of the previous year's less-satisfying performances will also be provoking me to go back to work.

My first action when this has happened each new year has been to track down Jack Grout and make a practice-tee date. Looking back, I can't remember ever failing to greet him with the same old line: "OK, Jack, let's go. Teach me golf all over again."

As I have described, in 1980 I almost literally meant what I said, and I did, indeed, learn a new golf swing. Normally what I have been requesting of Grout is a full review of the fundamentals. So important have these been to me throughout my career that I find it psychologically impossible to begin serious preparation for a new season without a complete review of them.

Sometimes that review has lasted an hour, sometimes a day, sometimes longer, depending on the cricks and creaks I've developed that violate Jack's ideas of proper form. And, without

fail, every year, predictable as sunrise, we have begun with the grip—and not moved on until both of us were 100 percent happy with it.

Does that surprise you—Jack Nicklaus taking lessons in how to hold the club after more than 30 years of playing golf? Well, let me amplify a little—and perhaps surprise you even more.

My basic grip pattern hasn't changed since I was a kid. However, I'm not a machine. Small variations in the way I hold the club can occur, especially after a layoff, or as an involuntary reaction to a flaw in some other part of my game (for instance, I needed to make a slight grip revision to go with my new swing pattern). This is true for all golfers, including names you see in headlines every week.

In my case, even a slight grip variation can make the difference between shooting 65s and 75s—or, if it becomes too ingrained, the difference between a lousy year and a great one. Because I can't see myself holding and swinging the club, such a variation is often extremely hard to detect. Thus, I resort to the year-opening review with Jack Grout, which is followed by further checks when necessary as the season develops.

Obviously, a person has to have his or her sights set pretty high to go to these lengths. But the point I am trying to make here, at the opening of this book, is that whether you want to win the Grand Slam or simply break 100 once a week, you will swing a golf club only as well as you hold it.

The grip is the foundation of the golf swing. Build it solidly and there is almost no limit to how well you might play this game. Construct it poorly and, just like a house, your problems with the rest of the structure will be endless.

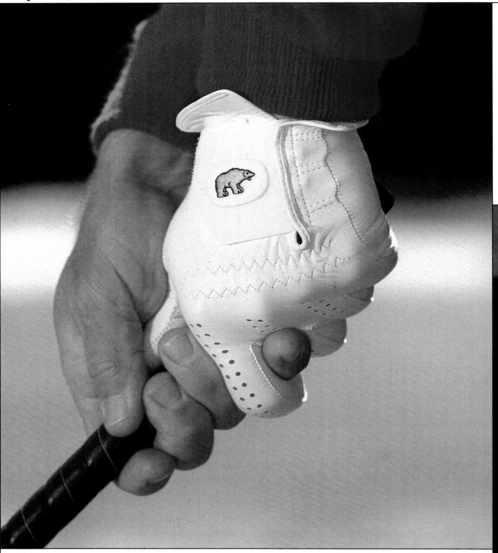

When we spell out what a golf grip must achieve to be 100 percent effective, it becomes obvious why all fine players and teachers have so belabored this point throughout the game's history.

A golfer has built himself a proper grip only when it:

1. promotes the proper clubface alignment and clubhead path away from and back to the ball,

2. allows the wrists to hinge or cock naturally and in the correct plane in response to the momentum of the clubhead during the backswing,

3. releases the clubhead into the ball at max-

imum speed in *reactive*—i.e., involuntary— response to the centrifugal force created by the downswing.

4. withstands the shock of impact without the hands slipping.

Hand placement or alignment, hand pressure and hand unification are the three factors that together determine how effectively the grip meets those goals. None seem to come naturally, particularly for late-starters or people who have never excelled at other bat-and-ball games. Thus, pa-

tience plays a critical part in mastering this first fundamental.

But the options are plain if the present foundation of your swing isn't up to par. Either acquire the knowledge, take the time and make the effort to rebuild that foundation, or resign yourself to playing golf below your potential for the rest of your life.

Unfortunately, it really is that simple—and that hard—a decision.

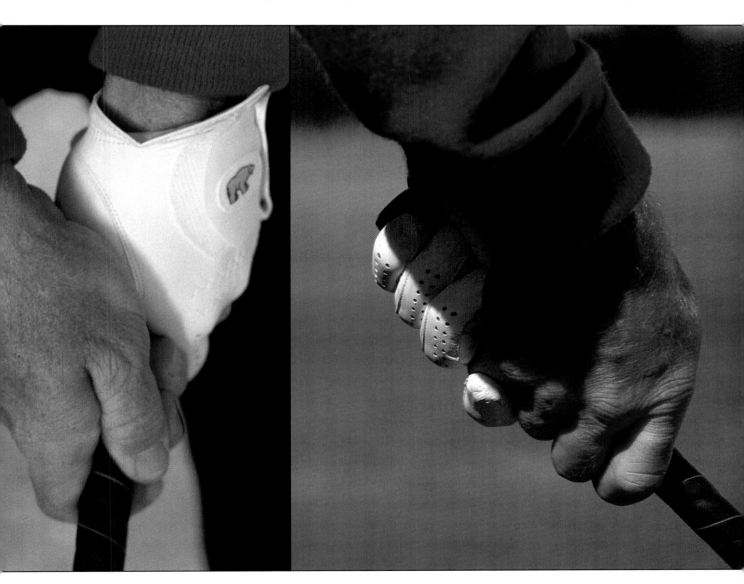

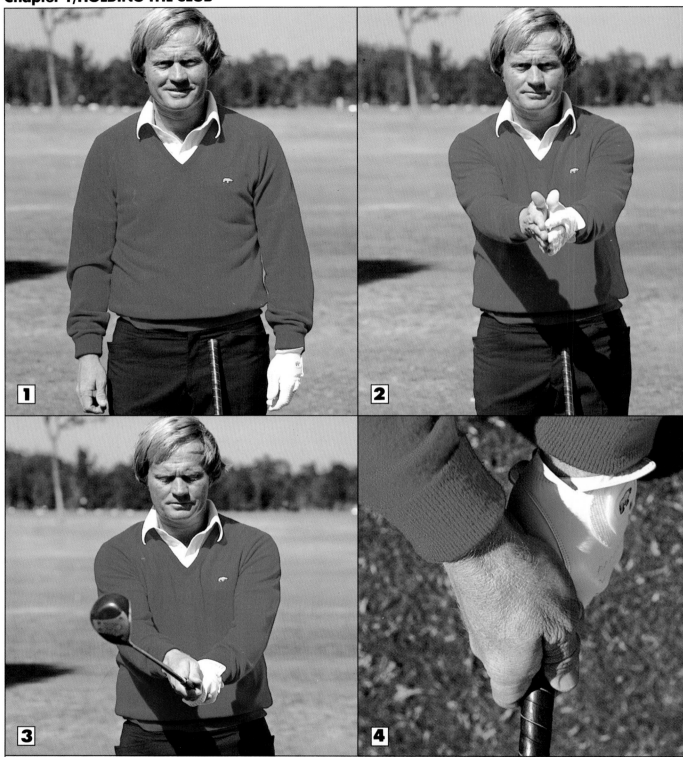

Aligning your hands

Assembling a fine golf grip doesn't require a Ph.D. in physics, but it does help if you know a little about cause and effect in the golf swing. Most important is an understanding of the effect that hand alignment has on clubface alignment.

If you hold the club with your hands turned well to the right as you set the clubface squarely behind the ball, more often than not the clubface will arrive back at the ball closed, or looking left of target, causing a pull or hook, depending on your swing path. Conversely, if you hold the club with your hands turned well to the left at address, most of the time you will strike the ball with the face open, or looking right of target, causing a push or slice.

The reason is the same in both cases. Human reflexes being what they are, when you make a golf swing your hands instinctively seek to return to a perpendicular plane as they apply club to ball. A few fairly good players have been able to fight this with compensatory maneuvers and much practice, but their careers invariably have been both inconsistent and brief. I believe a much better way is to master a grip that allows you to do what comes naturally.

Jack Grout taught me how to begin forming such a grip very simply at an early age. He called it "The Handshake," and I demonstrate it here. All it really involves is standing erect with your arms hanging easily at your sides, then extending each hand and wrapping it around the club aligned as it naturally arrives there.

Begin to form your grip this way and you will find that you set your hands on the club pretty much perpendicular to both the back of the ball and to each other. The more nearly you can maintain this relationship, the better your grip will meet all four of the goals outlined previously, but particularly the third—squaring the clubface at impact *reactively*.

If you must modify this grip, do so cautiously, a little at a time, being guided by the behavior of the ball. If it flies on a straight line to the right or curves right on most long shots, you are setting your hands too far to the left. If the majority of your full shots fly straight left or curve left, you are overdoing it the other way.

Especially avoid setting the hands on the clubs turned too far to the right. This gives many amateurs an illusion of strength, but, in my experience, the "stronger" a golfer's grip the weaker his swing will be.

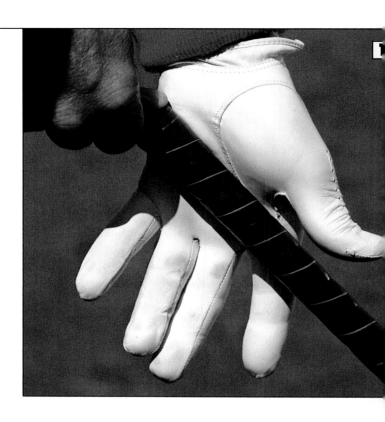

Setting your leading hand

Golf to me is a two-handed game, with both hands jointly performing a specific task. Essentially, I feel I direct and control the swing with my leading hand, the left, and transmit the power with my trailing hand, the right. Those roles determine how I set and secure the club in each hand.

I have been told that I accelerate the driver from rest at the top of the backswing to more than 100 miles per hour at impact in less than a quarter of a second, and apply almost a ton of force to the ball. If the leading hand is going to direct that kind of energy precisely, and withstand the shock of delivery without slipping, it had better be pretty solidly affixed to the club at the outset.

I achieve the necessary security by placing the club deeply enough into the palm of my left hand to be able, when I close my fingers, to wedge it very securely against the heel pad. This sense of palming and wedging with the leading hand is so important to me that, despite having small hands, I use slightly oversized grips on all my clubs.

The size and strength of your hands will influence what proportions of palm and fingers work best for you in setting the swing-controlling, shock-absorbing hand, and you shouldn't hesitate to experiment to find the best combination.

Keep in mind that the more you palm the club, the less your wrists will hinge or cock during the swing, which can cost you distance and promote slicing by reducing clubhead speed and leaving the clubface open at impact. Conversely, gripping more in the fingers can speed up both the clubhead and the closing of the face by enlivening the wrist action—but at the risk of hooking.

Incidentally, if the tips of your fingers dig into the heel of your leading hand as you complete the grip, you are either over-palming or you need built-up grips.

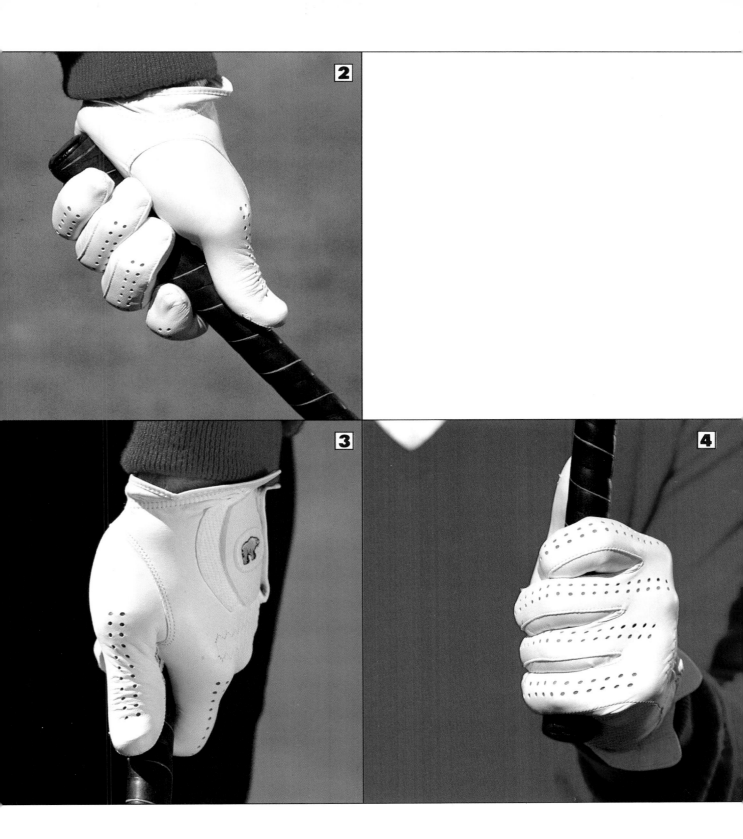

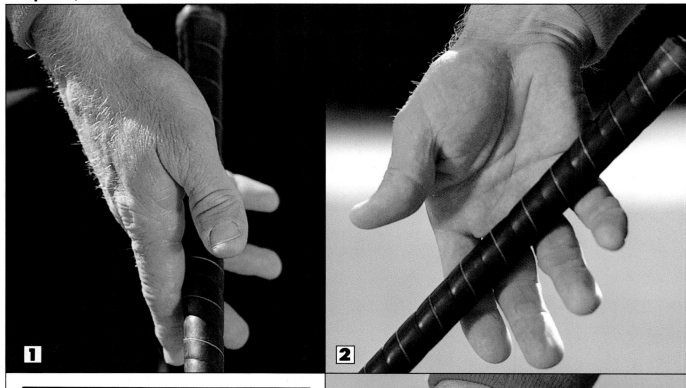

Setting your trailing hand

Place a golf ball in the palm of your trailing hand and see how far you can throw it. Note how much effort is required to move it a comparatively short distance. Now place a ball in your fingers and throw again. You will get at least twice the distance for less than half the effort—and throw a lot straighter, too.

Simply visualizing or sensing those two throws ought to explain why all good golfers, probably since the game was invented, have held the club *predominantly in the fingers* of the trailing hand. In a good golf swing the downswing is a race between the uncoiling of the body and the delivery of the clubhead by the arms, wrists and hands—the shot being perfectly "timed" when they tie at impact.

Palm the club in your trailing hand and it is physically impossible to apply it fast enough to achieve a dead heat. You will apply the clubhead late and lifelessly and with the face open, usually with an out-and-over shoulder lurch. The result invariably is a short, wild slice.

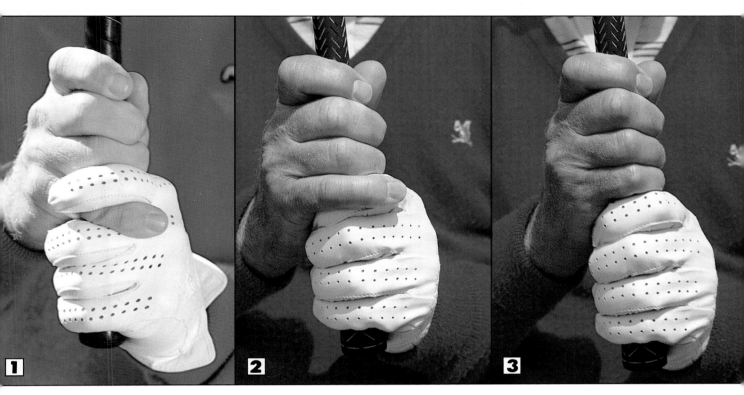

"Marrying" your hands

It is extremely difficult to hit a golf ball hard and true if your hands fight each other during the swing. Setting them parallel to each other helps unify their action. Setting them as close together as possible helps even more.

"Togetherness" is particularly important in terms of clubhead speed. To prove this to yourself, swing a baseball bat hands-together as though going for a homer, then make a hands-apart bunting stroke. The farther apart you set your hands in swinging any implement two-handed, the slower its striking end will travel.

I "marry" my hands by intertwining the little finger of the right hand under and around the base of the first finger of the left hand. This is known as the interlocking grip. I use it for three reasons. First, I started with it when I began to play golf and progressed rapidly enough at the game to see no reason to change. Second, having comparatively small hands, I get a better sense of compactness with the interlock than with the overlap or the 10-finger grip. Third, actually knitting a couple of fingers together gives me the best sense of hand

security and unity at all points in the swing.

Let me emphasize, however, that my method of uniting the hands is purely an idiosyncracy. By far the most popular grip is the overlap, first popularized by Harry Vardon almost a hundred years ago, in which the little finger of the right hand rides atop the first finger of the left. Some very fine golf has also been played with all 10 fingers on the club, as in gripping a baseball bat. Your choice should depend solely on which of the three styles best secures and unifies your hands at all points in the swing.

Consider the size of your hands in building or changing your grip. People with large hands or long fingers seem to find the overlap most effective. The majority of the good golfers who have used the interlock seem to have had small hands and/or chubby fingers. Not many top players have favored the 10-finger grip, probably because it encourages the right hand to become too dominant, but I've heard it can help those with weak hands.

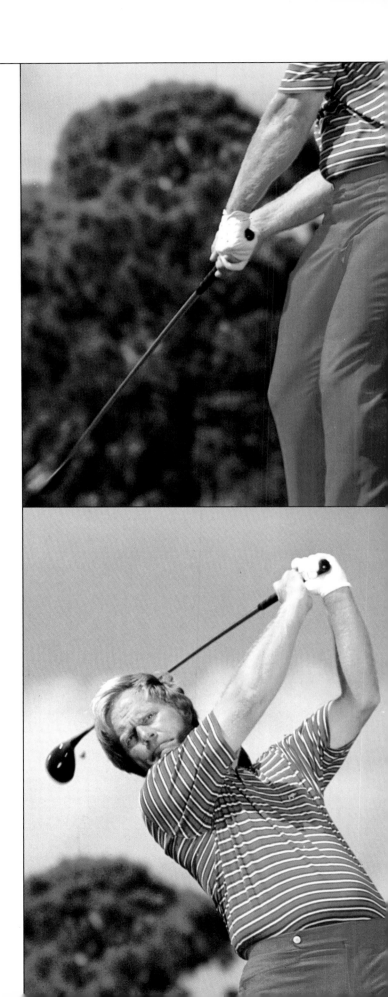

The proper grip pressure

Grip pressure is a gray area for most good golfers. For example, a skilled shotmaker will instinctively hold the club a little more lightly when trying to throw the ball extra high because a lighter grip promotes livelier use of the wrists, hands and clubhead. Conversely, when playing a low shot an expert golfer might hold on more firmly as an aid to delaying the clubhead and thereby delofting the clubface. For much the same reasons, the expert might grip a little firmer for a fade, in which the clubface must arrive slightly open, than he would for a draw when it must arrive slightly closed.

Such nuances aside, I suspect my grip pressure shades toward the firm, rather than the relaxed, end of the spectrum. I have a big swing, driven for most of my career much more by my legs and torso than my arms and hands. I have small and not particularly strong hands, and I have a definite horror of allowing the club to slip or turn in my hands at any point in the swing from takeaway to completion of follow-through. All those factors inspire secure adhesion to the club, especially in the left hand, which I feel directs and controls the swing.

Obtaining this security requires, in my case, the full use of both hands to hold the club—I dislike the thought that either might play hooky. Some parts of each hand, however, obviously exert more pressure than others.

In the left hand I exert the maximum pressure in my last two fingers, which wedge the club solidly against the heel-pad. In the right hand, I once felt that the thumb and forefinger carried some part of the load. In recent years I've decided that the two middle fingers should do most of the gripping—to the point, in fact, of hardly holding onto the club at all with the thumb and forefinger. Most fine players, I think, would have much the same sensations, which means they are good guidelines for all golfers.

A note of warning here: firm does not mean tight. The pressure of my grip is secure enough that you would have to apply a fair amount of force to pull the club from my hands, but I don't grab it like I would a snake I was trying to strangle. If firmness gets to a point where the veins on the back of your hand begin to bulge and your forearm muscles start to cramp, you are gripping way too tightly.

A moment ago I mentioned holding the club securely from the takeaway to the end of the follow-through. I find this vitally important because, for me, any movement of the club in the hands will be reflected in the clubface alignment at impact, and therefore in the flight of the ball. I know there have been some outstanding golfers who regripped the club at some point in the swing and delivered it to the ball as intended, but I'm not that talented. Also, I like to keep the compensations and margins for error at an absolute minimum in every aspect of my game.

Is grip security from takeaway to the completion of the follow-through carrying things a little too far? Well, it's true that a driver is in contact with the ball for only half a thousandth of a second and travels only three-quarters of an inch with the ball actually "on" the clubface, which means you surely can't change what's happening to a golf shot with your follow-through.

On the other hand, it's also true that your reflexes are not always subject to your will. If you get into the habit of relaxing your hands after impact, you might eventually begin to relax them before impact, especially when you consider how little time is involved—a few milliseconds.

I prefer not to take that chance.

Amateurs seem to suffer two particular problems related to grip pressure: grabbing the club early in the backswing and letting go of it at the top.

Grabbing can be a reaction to holding too lightly at address, but more often is the product of improper body action—an involuntary effect of lifting rather than turning the club back and up. Letting go at the top is sometimes a reaction to gripping too tightly at address, but usually is again a "cheap" or lazy way of trying to compensate for insufficient body turn in the backswing.

We'll see how both those problems can be licked when we get into the swing itself.

Chapter 2

Targeting

If you don't aim the gun properly you won't hit the bull's-eye

Stand directly behind the professionals at a tournament and you won't see many dead-straight drives—or even long approach shots that are perfectly straight, come to think of it. At first, many of the shots may look straight, but watch carefully and most of the time as the ball loses its forward impetus you will notice at least a slight drift to left or right.

This is deliberate, for three reasons:

First, to win in the big leagues your swing and your shot pattern must be both predictable and repetitive. The hardest shot to predict and repeat is the dead straight shot. In fact, particularly with the driver, the margins for error are so fractional that it's almost a miracle when a golfer does nail one straight as a string.

The second reason that top golfers mostly either draw or fade the ball is a matter of instinct. As a good player develops, he will gradually come to favor one curve or the other simply because the swing pattern that produces it seems for him the most natural or reliable, and thereby inspires the most confidence. Generally, a short hitter or a distance-conscious player will tend to draw the ball because of the extra yardage it offers. Conversely, a naturally powerful or accuracy-conscious golfer might prefer a fade because of the higher-flying and softer-landing shots it

promotes, which are invaluable scoring tools.

The third reason for "working" the ball, as we call it on tour, is a matter of percentages.

Aim down the center of the fairway or at the middle of the green and fail to hit straight and you can find yourself in trouble either to the left or the right. Aim down one half of the fairway, or at one side of the green, and, with a draw or fade, you are always working the ball toward the fat of the target. If the shot fails to curve and you hit it straight, you're still likely to catch the short grass or a piece of the putting surface.

When you can draw or fade a golf ball predictably and repetitively, you, in effect, block out one side of the golf course. If you are playing for titles or dollars, you had better comprehend and employ all such advantages.

I raise these factors as we begin to talk about targeting because they influence how a good player aligns the clubface and himself at address. Most of the time he isn't planning to travel, as it were, directly from north to south, but to get there slightly via west or east. At address, he sets the club and his body accordingly.

We'll look further into this later. Until then, it will make things a whole lot simpler if we assume I am not trying to curve the ball but am planning to hit every shot dead straight.

In many ways, playing a golf shot is like firing a gun. To shoot straight, you first have to hold the gun properly, then you have to aim it correctly. It's the same with a golf club. Unfortunately, an awful lot of amateurs want to be quick-draw artists—whip out the club and whack the ball, and to heck with all that grip and set-up baloney. That's fine if you're out there for fresh air and friendship, but forget about playing golf if that's your attitude. You might play *at* golf, but you won't come anywhere near the game I know.

Despite the fact that I'm one of the fastest walkers between shots on the tour and make a point of doing much of my surveying while others are doing theirs, some fans still regard me as a slow player. What they are noticing is the time I take in targeting and setting up to the ball. I am about as methodical and meticulous at those tasks as it is possible to be. That isn't going to change. I believe these are the most important factors in the entire game and I am psychologically incapable of shortcutting them.

Whether you are a Tom Watson or a Watts Thomson, if you don't aim the gun properly you won't hit the bull's-eye. You can't see yourself setting up to a golf shot, so if you don't work at targeting—patiently and consistently—you will not aim the gun properly most of the time. That's why *every* session I have with Jack Grout includes an aim-and-alignment check, usually before we look at any other part of my game.

Targeting involves five specific tasks:

1. Visualizing the shot.
2. Establishing the proper reference lines relative to the target.
3. Approaching the ball.
4. Aiming the club.
5. Aiming the body.

I intend to take all the time necessary to cover each in detail for you.

Visualizing the shot

You need a highly disciplined imagination to play good golf. Give your imagination free rein when in a position to win and it can be the death of you, especially if you let it wander into the future. Yet fail to use your imagination constructively in planning each shot and you will rarely if ever be in a position to win.

I am not an especially introspective individual, yet, by training, I have developed a very lively imagination when it comes to selecting golf shots.

I can ''see'' all my options in my mind's eye during the process of choosing a shot. Once the choice is made, I then try to visualize the flight of the ball to the target even more vividly before I step up to it (a picture that won't focus sharply is usually a warning to back off and reconsider). Next, I try with equal intensity to visualize the swing I need to make to execute the shot I have pictured. Only after these three mental exercises do I step up to the ball.

Establishing your target line

I attempt to hit every golf shot to a specific area of either fairway or green—sometimes even a specific spot. I don't always succeed, of course, but the exercise is important because of the positive focus it brings to both my mental visualization and my physical targeting procedure. In my experience, the more vaguely a golfer aims and aligns, the more vaguely he will swing.

The basic reference line in targeting for me is the direct line from the ball to my selected landing area or spot. If I intend to hit the ball dead straight, I will need to aim the clubface directly down that line and align my body exactly parallel to it. If I wish to fade or draw the shot, the direct ball-to-target line will provide the reference for the necessary angling of the body and clubface. Thus, accurately identifying and visualizing the direct ball-to-target line is critically important, no matter what type of shot I plan to play.

Most amateurs seem to begin looking for this critical line from a side-on perspective *after* they have begun to address the ball. Perhaps they have good enough eyesight or sense of direction to do so accurately. I don't. The only way I can establish an accurate image of the direct ball-to-target line in my mind's eye is from *behind* the ball, looking directly over it to the target.

Even then I don't trust myself to still "see" this all-important line accurately, once I have moved to the side of the ball, without a more immediate reference point. Thus, while standing behind the ball looking straight over it to the target, I select a mark—a leaf, twig or blade of grass—on the ground about 10 feet ahead of the ball directly on the target line. As I complete the setup, I then use this mark as my final checkpoint for both clubface and body alignment. I can't remember when I last hit a shot for real without doing this.

Almost all tour players "sight" their shots initially from directly behind the ball, and more and more also seem to be adding the close-up checkpoint routine.

Try both if you seem to be swinging well but miss the target a lot of the time.

Approaching the ball

The eyes can do strange things in lining up a golf shot. Step up from the side and, even if you have perfect vision, clearly visualizing the true ball-to-target line becomes much more difficult than from a position directly behind the ball.

Check this out sometime by first finding what you think is the line from the side of the ball, then take another look from squarely behind it. I think you will discover that your impressions of the line differ more often than they match.

This is why almost every good golfer moves into the address position as much as possible from directly behind the ball, rather than from an oblique or side-on angle. This creates a sharp mental impression of the basic reference line by looking directly over the ball to the target. The more closely you can continue to track that line visually as you move into the shot, the better impression of it you will retain as you finally move to the side of the ball.

I circle into position from directly behind the ball with the club in my right hand. I then place my right foot roughly in position first, followed by my left foot. As I add the left hand to the club and make my grip, I sweep my eyes through my short marker to the target and back by swiveling my head without my shoulders rotating (a common fault of poor players).

As I complete my stance, clubface aim and body alignment, and waggle the club a time or two, the short marker becomes more and more my key reference point. One last check on the short marker when all components of the setup are in place, and I am ready to pull the trigger—confident that the gun is at least aimed correctly, even if it should then misfire.

Aiming the club

To fly dead straight, a golf ball must be struck with the clubface looking momentarily directly at the target and the clubhead traveling momentarily directly along the target line. Any deviation in either face alignment or path, however slight, will produce a proportionate deviation in the ball's flight.

This is one reason I recommend that most golfers aim the bottom line of the clubface squarely at the target at address, though better players don't always do so even when attempting to hit the ball dead straight.

Until a person becomes expert at golf, the percentages are in favor of him instinctively reproducing at impact whatever angles he establishes at address. Thus a square clubface at the outset definitely improves the average player's chance of a square clubface at impact.

A second persuasive reason for setting the clubface squarely is the way its angle at address affects body alignment.

Most golfers will instinctively arrange themselves square to the facing of the club. This means that they will line up to the left of the target if they address the ball with the clubface closed, or to the right if they lay it open. By aiming the clubface squarely at the target, most players thus greatly enhance their chances of aligning themselves squarely, if only by adding a real reference line to the imaginary ball-to-target line.

These three views of club-ball alignment show my clubface set slightly open or to the right of the target, a preference I've developed over a lifetime. But until you can consistently control your ball-flight, I recommend aiming the bottom edge of the club square or perpendicular to the target.

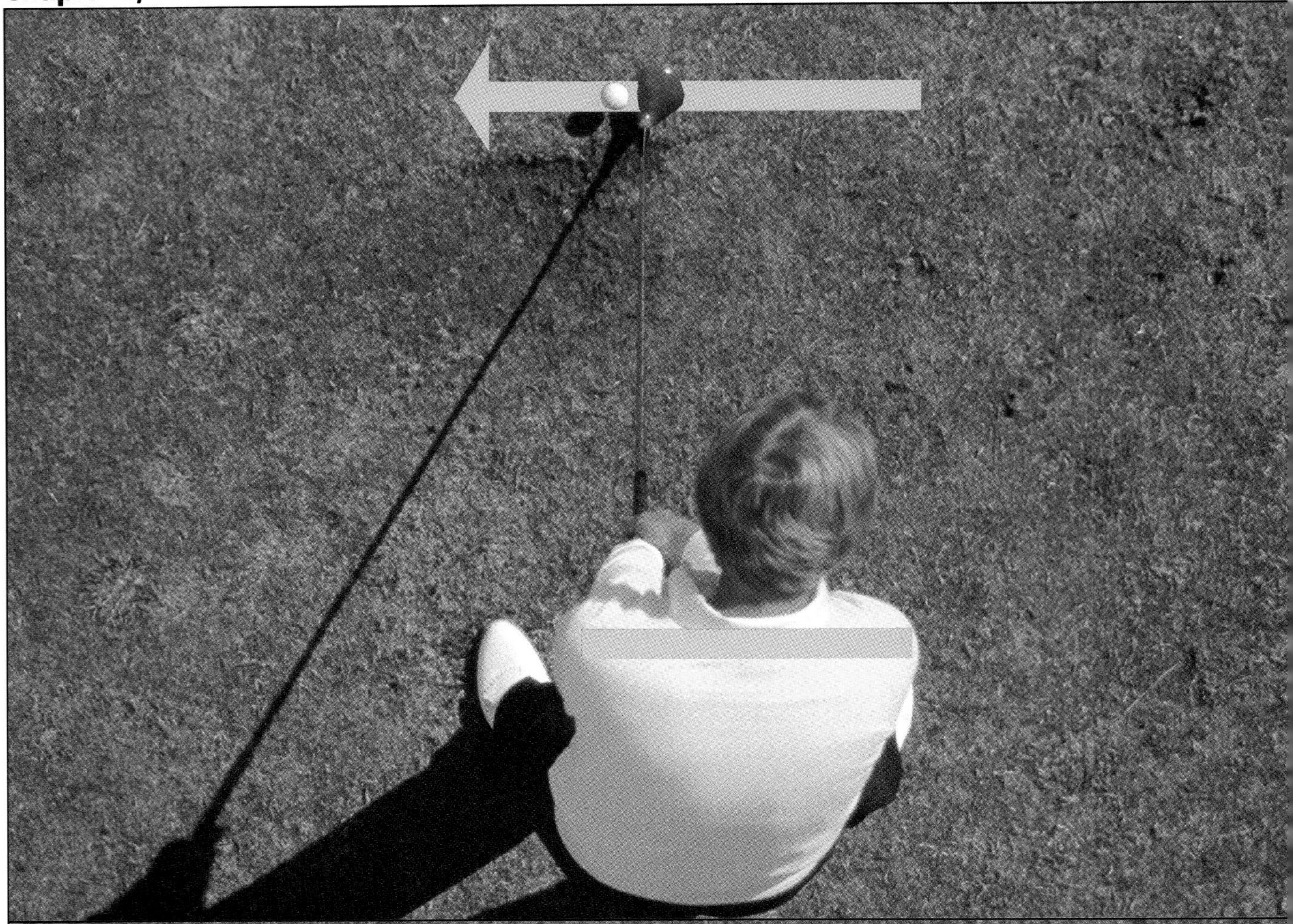

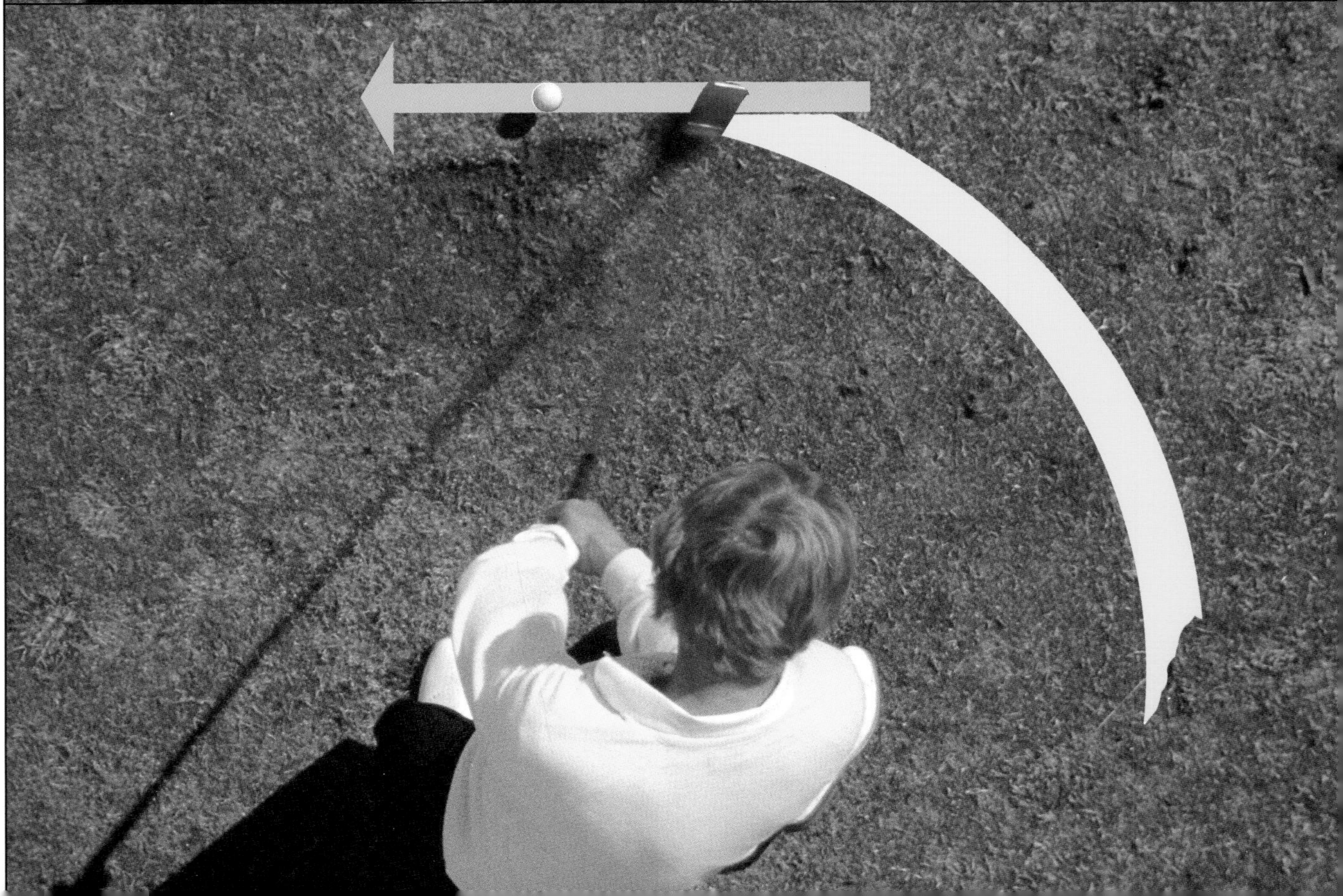

Aiming your body

One of the most challenging—and intriguing—aspects of the golf swing is its lack of absolutes. There are almost no blacks and whites in this game, only shades of gray. Identify what seems to be a rule applicable to all players and a moment later you will think of a fine golfer—sometimes even one of the game's great champions—who breaks it. Perhaps the only absolute is this one: if it works, use it.

Body aim or alignment is a particularly good example of the absence of standardization among skilled players.

In theory, if you aim yourself left or open to the target, you will fade or slice. Conversely, if you aim right or closed to the target, you will draw or hook. But at any tour event or amateur championship you can see plenty of golfers who align their bodies a little to the left and consistently draw the ball, and quite a few who align a shade to the right and fade most of their shots. Look carefully and you will also see that, in some instances, the alignment of the lower and upper halves of the body—particularly the feet and shoulders—don't

match. A dramatic example is Lee Trevino, who sets himself pretty much square from the waist up and wide open from the waist down.

That's absolutely fine if it's what works the best for a particular individual. In my case it doesn't, so I favor a more simple approach.

To fly the ball straight to the target, the path of the club at impact must exactly match the direct ball-to-target line. Most golfers, unless they have deliberately learned to do otherwise, will instinctively swing the club through impact traveling on a line square or parallel to a line through their shoulders. Also—unless again some other type of maneuver has been ingrained—most golfers will instinctively return their shoulder line at impact to whatever alignment it occupied at address.

Thus, if you don't make too many strange maneuvers during the swing, it seems to me that the more square your shoulders are at address, the more likely you are to deliver the clubhead along the proper path at impact. During 30 years of play I have found that it is easier to achieve shoulder squareness at both address and impact when the rest of the body is pretty much the same way.

I think most other golfers will, too.

By aligning my body square or parallel to the target line at address (upper photo), I find it much easier to return the club from inside that target line and square it up at impact (lower photo).

Chapter 3

Addressing the ball

Ball positioning—a way to simplify the game

Golf is among the most complex of games, so anything you can do to uncomplicate it is worth pursuing. The positioning of the ball offers such an opportunity. Get it right and a lot of good things will happen. Get it wrong and you sentence yourself to an endless chain of mishits and swing manipulations.

Proper ball positioning becomes a lot easier for all types of shots when it is based on a clear comprehension of impact "geometry"—of how the club must travel to the ball to meet it squarely and solidly. To achieve this, it helps to visualize the ideal arc and path of the clubhead through impact from two angles: looking at the golfer directly face-on but from ground level, as a worm might see him, and looking perpendicularly down on the ball as a bird might see him.

Seen from the worm's-eye view, perfect impact occurs when the center of the clubhead meets the equator of the ball exactly at the lowest point of the club's arc. When that happens, maximum force is applied to the back of the ball at the perfect angle relative to the loft of the clubface. Catch every shot like that and you would get a great feeling in your hands, fine distance, an optimum amount of backspin and possibly some thoughts about entering the Open.

When the ball is teed high, as for the driver, contact at the very bottom of the swing arc is a feasi-ble goal, first because there is small risk of catching ground before ball, and second because impact slightly before or after the base of the arc still produces an effective shot.

Unfortunately, when the ball is sitting on the ground, meeting it precisely at the bottom of the arc becomes too difficult for even the finest golfers. Catch the ground just fractionally before the ball, or the ball just slightly on the upswing, and the shot is wrecked. When the ball is grounded, therefore, we must settle for a compromise. The compromise is to strike the ball *slightly* before the clubhead reaches the bottom of the arc.

Let's now consider the bird's-eye view of the clubhead path, looking perpendicularly down on the ball as it is hit.

Despite what you may have heard or read or imagined to the contrary, a golf club cannot be swung effectively directly along the target line for more than a very short distance. Trying to deliver the clubhead from "in to *along*" the target line might be a useful corrective swing feeling for a habitual out-and-over player. Anyone, however, who actually kept the club on the target line for more than a millisecond would hit the ball very short distances and frequently into the tall weeds—not to mention wrench a few muscles with such a strained and artificial action.

The correct path of a golf club through impact for a straight shot is from *inside the target line, to momentarily along it, to inside again*—an ellipse, not a straight line. You can see this clearly in the overhead photos of me swinging through impact. Take my word that this is the proper clubhead path with every stick in the bag except, possibly, the putter.

It follows that for the ball to be hit straight it

must be positioned at the point where the center of the ellipse described by the clubhead coincides with the target line.

Position the ball back of that point and the clubhead must contact it while still traveling from inside the line, starting the shot right of target. Position the ball forward of that point and the clubhead must meet it while traveling back to the inside from *outside* the target line, starting the shot left. Many of the foul balls and ugly swing manipulations by middle and high handicappers spring entirely from such ball misplacement.

Where exactly should you then locate the ball to most often meet these two impact goals?

For me, the ideal position with my new swing has become opposite the inside edge of the left heel with the driver, and slightly back of that for all other normal shots. Depending on your type of swing and your skill level, yours could be anywhere from opposite your left big toe to as far back as the center of your stance. The only way to determine proper ball positioning for sure is by experimenting patiently and thoughtfully, always being guided by the starting direction, shape and trajectory of your shots.

Make the effort to do this experimenting if you are serious about golf, because proper ball positioning will greatly simplify the game for you.

Positioning the ball more toward the center of your stance for an iron shot (upper photo) insures a more descending arc and crisper contact. Positioning the ball opposite the inside of the left heel for a driver shot (lower photo) lets you sweep through the ball on a level or ascending arc.

To insure a descending blow with my irons (left), I position
the ball about an inch inside my left heel. When setting
up with a driver (right), the ball is off my left instep.

Guaranteeing a descending blow

You will produce your best shots with every club except the driver when you hit slightly *downward* through the ball.

The only way to achieve this is by leading the clubhead with the hands through impact. Allow the clubhead to overtake the hands even a smidgeon before contact and you risk hitting either "fat" (ground before ball) or "thin" (impact too high on ball). Permit the clubhead to really get out in front of your hands and your game will feature a succession of complete stubs and/or cold tops.

Thankfully, very early in my learning days Jack Grout taught me an almost foolproof way of insuring a slightly downward hit, and one so easy to master and ingrain I've rarely needed to think about it since.

Jack began by demonstrating that as long as the ball is positioned opposite a point inside the left heel, at impact the left shoulder is always ahead of that point—always nearer to the target than the ball. Next, he showed me that, as a consequence, if the left arm and clubshaft form a straight line from the left shoulder to the ball at impact, the hands *must* be slightly ahead of the ball as it is hit—they can't possibly be any other place. Finally, golf being so reactive a game, he reasoned that a golfer gives him the best chance of achieving at impact this straight left arm-clubshaft/hands-leading relationship by establishing it at address.

I have set up habitually with my left arm and clubshaft in a straight line ever since for all normal shots, and I strongly recommend it as the simplest way of automatically insuring a slightly downward hit.

You'll also obtain three other benefits from addressing the ball this way.

First, it promotes a smooth one-piece beginning to the backswing with the left side of the body in control. Second, it establishes at address the shoulder tilt essential at impact to deliver the club from inside the target line, i.e., left shoulder slightly higher than right. Third, it encourages setting the right arm "under" or "inside" the left, again as it must be at impact to hit from the inside.

Hitting the driver at the bottom of the arc

The more downward the hit with a driver, the more the effective clubface loft is increased and thus the more backspin is imparted to the ball. The more backspin a golf ball carries, the higher it soars and the quicker it stops. That type of flight robs you of distance. Thus, unless you are a Fuzzy Zoeller or a Tom Weiskopf, your objective when driving should be to catch the ball either at the very bottom of the swing arc or very slightly on the upswing.

Locating the hands even with the ball at address, rather than ahead of it, helps to pre-establish those types of impact. By keeping my left arm and clubshaft always in a straight line I am able to reposition my hands as required with only one small adjustment.

In setting up with the driver I move the ball forward in my stance, from about one inch inside my left heel to opposite its inner edge, while I move my hands only about half that much forward of their normal address position. As can be seen by comparing the photos at address with a long iron and the driver, this simple maneuver brings my hands pretty much even with the ball.

A similar adjustment might add a bit more oomph to your drives.

Distancing yourself from the ball

Stand too close to the ball at address and your swing arc will be better suited to splitting logs than fairways. Stand too far away and you'll fight a continual—and losing—battle with balance.

Both are common faults among amateurs, especially stretching or reaching for the ball. That's too bad because, once you know how, nothing in golf is easier than correctly distancing yourself from the ball.

Here's the method I learned as a kid and still use today should I become concerned about this element of my setup.

First, stand erect but "at ease," especially in the shoulders, with the club extended straight out in front of you at comfortable arm's length. Ensure that there is a slight natural break or concavity in your wrists. Flex your knees very slightly—just enough to take any tension or stress out of your legs—and stick your rear end out a little as you do so. Keep your head up, chin comfortably clear of your chest. Finally, without curving your back or dropping your hands, lean over from the hips, keeping them "up" as you do so, until the sole of

Stand erect but "at ease" (near right photo), with the club extended straight out in front of you. Then lean over from the hips until the club rests on the ground. This technique will position you the correct distance from the ball, from the driver (center photo) down to the sand wedge (far right photo).

the club rests lightly on the ground.

You are now the proper distance from the ball no matter which club you are holding. Using this measuring technique, you obviously will stand farthest from the ball with the driver and closest with the sand wedge, with progressive variations in between. That's exactly as it should be.

Be sure that your arms hang almost straight down, with the upper portions close to your chest. If your arms angle acutely forward, and/or separate entirely from your chest, you are too far from the ball.

Check that your left arm and the clubshaft dip only slightly beneath an imaginary straight line running from the top of your left shoulder to the top of the ball. If the dip is accentuated, you are too close to the ball. If there's no dip or, worse yet, your wrists are forced to arch upward, you are reaching—you are too far away.

Sense your weight distribution. Your weight should be equally distributed between the balls and heels of both feet for all normal full shots from a level lie. If your weight is mostly back on your heels, you're too close to the ball. If your weight is predominantly on your toes, you're too far away.

Establish your distance as I've described and you kill three birds with one stone by also achieving correct posture at the ball and preprogramming the proper swing plane relative to your height.

Placing your feet

The role of the feet in the swing—or more precisely, the feet and ankles—might just be the most neglected element in golf instruction. Their behavior is as crucial at every stage of the action as any other area of the anatomy, yet they frequently seem to get the least attention. Certainly, flat-footedness and wooden-leggedness are two of the biggest swing-cripplers I see among amateurs.

Perhaps one reason the feet are overlooked by many golfers is that, properly used, they operate as an effect, not a cause—in *reaction* rather than in response to conscious command. Knowing or sensing this, golfers assume that if they pay enough mind to other seemingly more important swing elements, their feet and ankles will respond correctly.

Unfortunately, that often is not the case. I'd say at least half the amateurs I encounter would substantially improve most other elements of the swing by first learning proper use of their feet and ankles. We'll talk more about that when we get to the swing itself.

As with so many swing components, correct foot and ankle action is pre-established at address.

Set your feet either too wide apart or too close together as you address the ball, and you'll have one heck of a job working them effectively during the swing. Likewise, incorrect angling of the feet and/or improper weight distribution will virtually assure faulty foot action during the swing, especially on the longer shots.

Finding your proper stance width

I learned to play golf from the *insides* of my feet by hitting thousands of balls while working only at shifting most of my weight to the insides of both feet going back, then retaining it there at least through impact solely by rocking my ankles. That was hard labor, but the "centeredness," balance and leg and ankle strengthening it produced have paid off enormously ever since.

You may not care to go to such lengths. Either way, you will strengthen your swing greatly by adopting a stance width that enables you to turn fully in the backswing without rolling to the outside of your right foot, and that doesn't force you onto the outside edge of your left before the ball is struck.

For most golfers, including me, that ideal occurs with the longest clubs when the feet are set apart about shoulder width at the centers of the heels.

If after some thoughtful practice this doesn't seem appropriate for you, experiment with slightly wider and slightly narrower stances, but don't overdo it. Too wide a stance can restrict your backswing turn, especially if your feet are inactive to begin with. The closer together the feet are set, the tougher it becomes to swing from their insides when making a full turn going back and a complete release coming down.

As the clubs shorten, requiring less backswing body turn and arm extension, most good players progressively narrow the stance to a point where, with the wedges, the heels are only a few inches apart. I effect this narrowing simply by moving the right foot closer to the left, which enables me to use the left foot as a constant reference for ball positioning.

You should do the same.

Maintain your weight on the insides of your feet at address, on the backswing and at least through impact, as I am doing here.

Distributing your weight

In talking earlier about establishing the correct distance from the ball, I suggested that the best distribution of weight for all normal full shots from a level lie is equally between the balls and heels of both feet and equally on both legs. Setting my weight thus has served me well for more than three decades, so I don't intend to change.

Theories about various elements of technique, however, do change as the golf swing continues to evolve, and for some years now a lot of fine teachers have been recommending that their less-skilled pupils favor the right leg a little more than the left in distributing the weight at address.

The idea here is that most recreational golfers, and particularly older late-starters, have difficulty shifting sufficient weight on to the right leg in the backswing to avoid ''reverse pivoting''—tilting toward the target instead of turning away from the target. The argument continues that, by setting more weight to the right at address, such a golfer gives himself, in effect, a running start at getting most of the weight to that side during the back-swing. This, in turn, the theory concludes, permits and encourages a proper shifting of the weight toward the target coming down.

My basic reaction to this: if it works, fine; use it and hang on to it. The only question I would raise concerns balance, which ultimately is perhaps the single most critical factor in the golf swing.

I may be unusual, but to feel that I will be fully balanced during the swing I must feel extremely well-balanced at address. I certainly don't want to feel anchored to the ground—a sense of resilience or springiness is vital to me. On the other hand, I do want to be very *stable* over the ball; stable enough that if someone were to give me a pretty good shove from any direction—front, rear, or either side—I would not fall off balance.

In my case, this sense of complete balance and stability only happens when I set my weight at address equally between the balls and heels of both feet and equally on both legs.

If you can achieve a sense of being fully and finely balanced otherwise, then go right ahead. I suggest, however, that you run a ''shove test'' before you make a final commitment.

I like to feel well-balanced at address (above) with my weight equally distributed between the balls and heels of both feet and equally on both legs. On most shots I try to set my left foot about 15 degrees open relative to the target line (right).

Angling your feet

On the tour we have golfers who can hit the ball kneeling down, or while sitting on a chair, or while standing on one leg—and well enough probably to break 80. Lift any of these players even a fraction of an inch off the ground, however, and they could not hit a golf ball at all.

You need *traction* to swing a golf club. Combined with stance width and weight distribution, the quality of a golfer's traction depends on the angling of his feet.

I know a few tour players who walk a little pigeon-toed or splay-footed, but I've never seen a great shotmaker stand to the ball either way. One reason is that both alignments force improper leg and body movements that severely inhibit a free swinging motion. Even more important, they make swinging in balance almost impossible.

Throughout most of the game's history, most good strikers have put balance ahead of all other considerations and protected it in the most natural way, by slightly toeing out both feet at address. That's a good starting point for everyone, and particularly for beginners.

As a golfer's swing improves, however, he might want to try two variations that in recent years have developed at the top levels of the game from increased use of the legs and body and less dependence on the hands and arms.

Observe the tour players as a group and you will see that most, including me, normally set the right foot at address pretty much square or at 90 degrees to the target line. The purpose of this placement is chiefly to put a brake on the backswing turn: it promotes control by reducing the possibility of overswinging when accuracy is more important than raw distance. I depart from this square rear-foot alignment only when going for all the marbles with the driver. Then, to permit increased body turning, I will sometimes angle my right foot a few degrees away from the target.

Left-foot alignment varies more than right-foot positioning among the best players, from angling just a few degrees outward to almost 45 degrees toward the target. You'll notice, however, that all fine golfers open or splay out the forward foot to some extent. The objective is the same in every case—namely to facilitate effective lower-body action on the forward swing while still retaining good balance.

On most shots I try to maintain a happy medium by setting the left foot about 15 degrees open relative to the target line. Depending on how my swing feels, I will sometimes increase that angle when going for a big drive as an aid to speeding up my leg drive and hip clearance. The danger here, however, lies in driving the legs and clearing the hips so fast that the shoulders are pulled around too quickly, which makes for a high slice or a hard pull, depending on the clubface alignment.

Experiment intelligently to find your own best angles.

You will find that the "squarer" you set your forward foot, the faster your hands and arms will deliver the clubhead to the ball relative to the unwinding of your lower body. This normally promotes a right-to-left flight pattern. Conversely, the more toward the target the foot is angled, the more your lower body will lead your arms, hands and clubhead through impact, which generally produces a left-to-right flight pattern.

For a number of years I positioned my head well behind
the ball (right), but since early 1980 I have centered my
head more (left) to help ``deepen'' my swing plane and
allow my arms to swing behind and less above my head.

Positioning your head

In all previous writings I have recommended setting the head well behind the ball for normal full shots, which is what I did myself for 30 years.

I had two primary reasons for this positioning. First, as I explained earlier, setting my head well back at address helped to prevent it moving toward the target on the forward swing, which is a sure shot-wrecker. Second, it allowed me to keep the full weight of my body behind the ball through impact, which I knew added power to my shots.

I can still see merit in those theories, especially for golfers prone to swinging their heads and upper bodies forward along with the clubhead. However, although my head is still behind the ball at address (and, of course, at impact), since early 1980 it hasn't been quite as far back as it was before that time.

This repositioning of the head was integral to the swing changes that I reviewed in the introduction to this book and will be explained in more detail later. Essentially, the repositioning came about as follows.

As I said in the introduction, by allowing my swing plane to become much too upright I had for a number of years experienced great difficulty in releasing the clubhead fully and solidly into the back of the ball. Essentially, the over-upright swing plane was forcing too steep an angle of clubhead approach through impact, causing the ball to be struck obliquely rather than drilled directly in the rear.

Flattening or—to use the word I think better describes my eventual cure—"deepening" the swing required, among other things, more turning and less tilting of the shoulders on the backswing. Further, because the plane of the swing is established by the first foot or two of motion, I had to find a way of turning more and tilting less, right from the moment the clubhead left the ball.

Jack Grout had been telling me for years that the farther behind the ball I set my head at address the more my arms were forced upward rather than rearward as I began the swing, and that the more upward the initial path of my arms, the more my shoulders would tilt and the less they would turn as the backswing progressed. Grout insisted, as we worked together in the early spring of 1980, that my head was now too far behind the ball.

Finally, thank goodness, I decided to really listen to him and resolved to give the more-centered head position a thorough trial, strange and uncomfortable as it felt at first. Pretty soon, turning rather than tilting my shoulders directly away from the ball began to feel a whole lot easier.

A week or so later, helped by some other changes we'll examine along the way. I could also feel my hands and arms beginning to match the deeper shoulder turn and thereby swinging more behind and less above me. Reflecting now on all of the changes I made, I'm sure none of them would have worked as well—if at all—without the new head position.

Is there a lesson here for you? Well, if you sense your swing is too upright, try centering your head a little more at address. Conversely, if you're too flat, try setting it more behind the ball.

And never be too stubborn when a trusted teacher thinks he sees a flaw!

Part Two
THE SWING

Chapter 4

Before you pull the trigger

Hang loose but lively

The next time you go to the practice tee, try this experiment. Prepare properly for a full shot. Then, with the address completed, tense as much of your body as you can as hard as you can. Really clench those muscles, especially in your hands, arms and legs. Now, without relaxing, try to make a golf swing. If you can swing at all you will find the action wooden, jerky, restricted, clumsy, lifeless. The ball, if you make contact at all, will fly short and probably in an unpleasant direction.

Then go to the other extreme. As you complete the address, let everything go limp and languid —really "hang loose." Now swing without allowing any return of tension anywhere in your body. The action will feel free and fluid, loose and limber. The ball will probably go farther than usual and maybe even where you intended it to.

The purpose of this little exercise is to prove to yourself the incredibly destructive effect of excessive muscular tension at the beginning of the golf swing. No matter how good your mechanics, if you can't get the swing started without gritting your teeth and knotting your muscles, golf is forever going to be a most punishing game.

Please note that I emphasize "get the swing started," not completed. It is obviously impossible to make a strong, controlled pass at a golf ball without a good deal of muscular contraction and expansion in various parts of the body as the action progresses. The trick is to start with the muscles as "quiet" as possible while still feeling ready for some lively action, then allow them to

work naturally and smoothly in reactive response to the swinging motion. "Relaxed springiness" is the best description I can offer of the way I most like to feel just before I draw the club back.

Regrettably, all this is an awful lot easier to talk about than to achieve. Tension is the product of fear, thus the less confident you are in your swing mechanics, your shotmaking judgments, your recovery powers, or any particular competitive situation, the more "tightly" you will start the swing.

I know it's tough medicine to swallow, but the only foolproof way to increase and sustain your confidence in all four of those areas is to get better at the game through study, tuition and practice.

If that sounds worse than a jail sentence, at least try to make the most of the purely physical aids to staying loose and lively that all good golfers employ in one form or another.

For example, you will rarely see a fine player become completely immobile at any point from beginning to set up to the ball to starting the swing. The reason is that the longer the muscles are "frozen," the tighter they become. Thus skilled golfers —indeed, skilled performers in all sports— have learned to always keep some part of themselves in motion in preparing for the main action.

This "antifreeze" motion takes many forms among tour golfers, but one almost universal expression of it is the waggle. Waggling the club excessively can be destructive by upsetting aim and alignment, but two or three loose and easy waggles are a great way to fight tension, especially in the hands and arms. Also, properly executed, the waggle is a valuable swing-rehearser, about which I'll have more to say in a moment.

Left: to prevent tightness in my upper body, I swivel my head to look from the ball to the target. Above: I've relearned the importance of keeping my grip pressure light.

Shuffling the feet throughout the setup procedure—a sort of ''walking-in-place'' motion—is another common tension-reliever, as are a slight flexing of the shoulders and arms or a soft ''milking'' of the club in the hands.

Talking of the hands, in recent years I've also relearned the importance of keeping the grip light immediately prior to and during the beginning of the swing. Too tight a grip pressure produces tension in the forearms, which in turn builds tension in the shoulders, and so on by chain reaction throughout the rest of the body. So treat the club gently: if its head doesn't feel ''heavy'' as you waggle, you're almost certainly gripping too tightly.

Whatever the maneuvers, you will notice that most good players continue them right up to the point of initiating the swing. Also, such moves tend to become more extended or pronounced in proportion to the degree of competitive pressure being experienced—an involuntary response to the muscle-tightening effects of nervous tension. Let that happen in your case, too—without, I hope, getting to the point of looking like a disco dancer.

Although I don't fidget an awful lot once I'm over the ball, I do employ a couple of by-now almost involuntary tension-relievers. These are a slight lateral rocking or shuffling of my legs and hips as I complete the address, combined with a probably imperceptible flexing or ''easing'' of the shoulders. Also, swiveling my head to look from the ball through my close-up check mark to the actual target and back again a number of times helps to prevent tightness in my upper body.

How you fight tension isn't terribly important, so long as it doesn't disrupt your aim and alignment. What *is* important is that you keep your muscles ''springily relaxed'' right up to the point where you pull the trigger.

To ground or not to ground?

Most good golfers begin the swing with the club grounded—its sole resting on the grass behind the ball. I do not. I begin every swing with the club held very slightly above ground, for a number of reasons.

First and foremost, keeping the club just clear of the ground helps me to avoid excessive tension, especially in the all-important hands and forearms. With the club grounded there is an inclination to press it downward. Quite apart from the possible illegality of such an action—are you or are you not improving the lie?—pressing the clubhead into the ground forces a muscular resistance that is bound to tighten first the hands and forearms and then, by chain reaction, most of the rest of the body.

Second, the more firmly the club is grounded, the tougher it is to swing it away from the ball smoothly and the greater the risk of stubbing it in the grass immediately back of the ball. As the beginning of the swing to me is one of its two absolute make-or-break points (the other being the change of direction), I try to avoid anything that might jeopardize the process.

Third, when you ground the club in rough or many types of loose material, you risk incurring penalties by causing the ball to move. Golf's tough enough without having to add strokes you didn't hit.

Fourth and finally, I find it easier when the club is not grounded to start back from the ball with all parts of my body working in unison. When I set the clubhead on the ground there is a tendency for my hands to get ahead of my body, probably as the result of feeling I have to "unplug" the clubhead with them as the initiating motion.

If you have ingrained beginning the swing with the club grounded, you might find it difficult at first to start back with it above ground. If you are fighting a losing battle with hand and forearm tension or starting back smoothly, however, then my technique might be worth a try.

Try it first on the practice tee beginning with a short iron, not in a competitive round beginning with the driver. And expect to have to apply some patience and some perseverance.

Center the clubface to the ball

Golf is a game of cause and effect, of action and reaction. Unless you ingrain corrective or compensatory moves, which needlessly add to the game's difficulty, you instinctively will mirror at point Z in the swing whatever you did at point A.

The golf swing has only two objectives. One is to create speed in the clubhead, which we'll look into a little later. The other is to deliver the center of its face square and flush to the back of the ball. I believe a golfer gives himself the best chance of achieving the second of these objectives when he begins the swing with the clubface and ball so related.

You will see exceptions to this on the tour. A few players address the ball opposite the heel of the club, and a few others set it out around the toe. Also, you'll see a number of golfers who allow quite a lot of daylight between clubface and ball at address. These are idiosyncrasies, developed and ingrained to compensate for some personal swing peculiarity. My advice is to learn whatever you can from other elements of those golfers' techniques but to ignore those particular ones.

Set the clubface where your instincts tell you and where they will most easily return it—centered and as close as you comfortably can get it to the back of the ball.

Keeping the clubhead clear of the ground (left) helps me avoid excessive tension in the hands and forearms. A few players address the ball opposite the heel or toe of the clubface, but I like to center the clubface to the ball (below) to give me the best chance of delivering the center of the clubface flush with the back of the ball.

Chapter 5

Starting back

A reminder and a warning

We are now a third of the way through this book and the club still hasn't moved away from the ball. I think that is a lesson in itself—and, indeed, one of the most important I can offer any truly improvement-conscious golfer.

When most people take up golf they want to go out immediately and swing the club and attack the course, and that's perfectly understandable. The trouble is that most, no matter how well they would like to play, never can subdue that initial urge sufficiently to actually learn *how* to do this.

Golf is really two games. The first is ball-striking, shotmaking—the physical side. The second is strategy, tactics, course management, self-management—the mental and emotional side. Unfortunately, nobody is a "born golfer" in either department. Some people may have more innate talent than others for one or both elements of the game, but how well a person ultimately plays depends on how well he or she *learns* both elements.

And, make no mistake, if you want to be a really fine player it's a long, hard process. I've been learning both games of golf now for more than 30 years, and I still see no end to the process.

I make this little pitch because here I want to remind you once again, as we begin to talk about the swing itself, that how effectively you swing a golf club depends *almost entirely* on how well you have *prepared* to do so. All the finest players learned early in their careers that the quality of the swing is dependent about 80 percent on preparation and 20 percent on execution. Reverse those proportions and you'll always be a hacker.

Asked what he thought about during the swing, Sam Snead once replied: "Nothing." Sam's about as close to a natural golfing genius as I've ever encountered, but I'm absolutely certain he would never have broken 80 without an awfully active mind immediately *before* he started the club back.

To be able to think of nothing during the swing itself is a marvelous goal for any golfer, because it indicates totally reflexive action stemming from perfect preparation. And consider this. Your reflexes may never allow you to swing as well as Sam, but there's nothing to stop you from learning how to *prepare* to do so as well as he does, because preparation requires no complex motion and therefore no reflexive action.

Too much trouble? Well, what would an 80 percent improvement in one-half of the game do for your scores, even if you never improved the remaining physical 20 percent, or one percentage point at golf's mental half?

End of reminder. Now for the warning.

Through many years of study, practice and play, I know pretty precisely what I do with each part of my body as I swing the club, and I'll try to describe fully those actions and reactions in what follows. However, never make the mistake of trying to actually swing in the step-by-step or part-by-part manner in which I'm obliged to analyze my swing here.

How well you swing the club depends almost entirely on how well you have prepared beforehand (above). Preparation requires no complex motion and therefore no reflexive action. An effective golf swing is above all else a continuous flow of motion (right). The less you try to dissect your swing while playing, the better the motion will be—and the better swing you'll make.

An effective golf swing is above all else a continuous *flow* of motion, and the less you need to dissect or direct it while actually playing the game, the better the motion will flow. Therefore, never work on more than one or at most two swing elements at a time, and do so always on the driving range, not when you're trying to make a score. In other words, avoid paralysis by analysis and ac-

cept the truth of the old tour adage that if you didn't bring it with you, you won't find it on the golf course.

Finally, if you decide to copy me, do so in principle but not necessarily in detail. No two people ever have swung a golf club identically and none ever will. You'll be wasting time and energy by even trying.

The importance of starting correctly

Some years ago my swing was timed along with those of a number of other golfers. From starting back to impact I took 1.96 seconds. Most of the other players were faster—around 1.5 seconds.

The scientists claim to have proved that human muscle-to-brain-and-back-to-muscle reactions simply aren't quick enough for a golfer to be able to consciously direct his entire swing in those amounts of time. They contend that once even the slowest-swinging golfer is about two-thirds of the way into his backswing, all the rest of what he does will be purely reflexive.

My own experience indicates they probably are right. At peak form I can sometimes save a shot with a small backswing adjustment, but I can seldom do that once I've begun to change directions. Either way, such a correction usually seems much more reflexive or instinctive than conscious-

ly directed, and it's definitely not a phenomenon I would care to rely on in tournament play. Generally, when I start the swing badly, the ball finishes badly.

The big lesson in this for me is that, when you swing a golf club, your actions are under full conscious control—can be fully mentally directed for certain—*only during the initial motion away from the ball.* To me, that makes the beginning of the swing an awfully darned important move.

Starting the swing correctly in my case involves correctly marrying four distinct but closely interrelated elements. They are (1) the flow of preparatory motion into swing motion, (2) the path of the clubhead and the clubface alignment, (3) the pattern of body action and (4) the pace or tempo of the initiating movement.

Let's look at each separately.

Making the motions flow

Earlier in this book I talked about the importance of staying slightly in motion as you prepare to swing, to help reduce tension. Smoothly blending whatever "antifreeze" motions you find most effective into your swing-triggering movements is the first key to a sound start. The *worst* thing you can possibly do is become totally immobile completing the setup and beginning the swing.

The most popular swing-triggering motion among good players is the forward press: a slight inclination of the hands and arms, or the hands and arms and body, toward the target, with the clubhead, in effect, recoiling away from the ball as the pressing motion reaches its forwardmost point. For much of my career this never suited me, partly because it always seemed to cause the clubface to open, and partly because it started the hands and clubhead back a little too much ahead of my arms and body.

In place of the conventional forward press, for

For me, the swiveling of my chin to the right serves two important functions—it helps to start my takeaway and it makes room for a full body turn on the backswing. I recommend it as long as you don't let it develop into a sway.

The correct takeaway, the initial motion away from the ball, is vital. Very rarely can I save a swing midway through the motion if I started it badly.

many years I used what I liked to call a "stationary press," this being simply a slight firming up of the grip just before I started the clubhead away from the ball. Combined with the increase in grip pressure, I also swiveled my chin away from the target to a point where I could see the ball only with my left eye.

I dropped the stationary press in the early '70s after discovering that for a number of frustrating years the increased hand pressure had been causing a slight closing of the shoulders as I began the backswing. In its place I adopted and have since used more of a regular forward press, easing my entire body very slightly toward and also a little left of the target—the latter to protect against starting back with the shoulders closed.

I ingrained the chin swivel in my earliest golfing days, both as a swing trigger and as a means of making maximum space for a full backswing body turn. I've continued to use it ever since and I recommend it to all golfers for both of those reasons.

Sam Snead has always used much the same motion for the same reasons I do, and you will notice it to a greater or lesser degree in the swings of many fine players. Its only danger lies in allowing the swiveling of the chin to grow into a swaying of the head and body, so guard against overdoing a good thing.

Clubhead path and clubface alignment

On the tour there are a number of very fine golfers who start the club back along one path and return it to the ball along another. Usually the club is started back to the outside of the target line, then pulled or dropped rearward at some point in the swing so that at impact it is arriving at the ball from the inside of the target line.

The word for this type of action is "looping," and if it works as well for you as it's worked, say, for Isao Aoki or Hubert Green, then I wouldn't want to talk you out of it. Golf truly is a game of how many, not how.

To my mind, however, changing swing paths in midstream has to be a hard way to play a game that demands repetition above all else, if only because of the added motion it brings to an already complex set of actions.

I have always sought to simplify golf as much as possible. Starting the club back from the ball as I want it to return is to me an important simplifier. That way I have to consciously direct the swing action only while I am in full mental control over it. Given a good start, I should be free thereafter to let things happen reactively.

As we noted earlier, to hit a golf shot dead straight the clubhead must meet the ball while traveling momentarily directly along the target line. It is important in getting the swing off to a sound start to understand that this all-important impact goal can only be achieved when the clubhead travels from *inside* the target line right up to the very millisecond it meets the ball. If the center of the clubhead passes even fractionally beyond the target line before impact, it *must* be traveling back across the line as the ball is struck—or from out to in, to use the common description.

That's physics pure and simple, and I suggest you never forget it.

How rapidly and how far a golf club swings to the inside of the target line going back depends primarily on the distance the golfer stands from the ball. This, in turn, depends on a combination of build and address posture and the length of the club being played.

To simplify the swing as much as possible, I want the club returning to the ball on much the same path it traveled on the takeaway. That means if I want the club swinging into the ball from inside the target line—and I do—I must let it swing naturally inside going back. When I do that, as these sequences of two swings from different angles indicate, it comes back down on the path I want. Changing swing paths in midstream seems to me to be a hard way to play a game that demands a high degree of repetition. Starting the club back the way it should return is one way to simplify the swing.

Essentially, the taller the golfer and the shorter the club, the closer he *naturally* will stand to the ball, thus the more gradually the club will *naturally* swing to the inside and the less far inside it *naturally* will have traveled at the completion of the backswing. The opposite is true, of course, for a shorter golfer playing the longer clubs.

Please don't miss the emphasis on *naturally* in all of this, because it is the key factor in achieving an *overall* sound swing pattern, as well as a correct initial swing path. Absolutely the *last* thing any golfer should do is to try to "take" or force the club to the inside by manipulating it in some way in the early stages of the backswing. More on that later.

A swinging door provides the best analogy I know for implanting a picture of the correct clubhead starting path, and an equally good picture for the alignment of the clubface during the early stages of the backswing.

As you open a door, it immediately begins and continues to swing on a consistent arc progressively more and more to the "inside" of the line of its nonsupporting jamb.

That's exactly the pattern for the ideal path starting back when attempting to hit the ball straight.

Now let's look at what ideally should happen to the face of the club as it begins its backward journey—which might just be the most confusing point in golf for a lot of high handicappers.

Swing the door again, but this time watch what happens to the plane of its outer edge as the motion proceeds.

What you will see is that the farther the door swings, the more the plane of its outer edge "opens" relative to the line of the jamb. What you will also see, however, is that the plane of the outer edge remains constantly at 90 degrees to the arc on which the door swings.

Or, as a skilled golfer would see and describe it, the outer-edge plane *remains constantly square to the arc of the swing*.

That's exactly what I want my clubface to do, not only as it leaves the ball but all the way to the completion of the backswing.

If this is not already a goal of yours, I believe you will play better by making it one.

Getting it going all together

In golf there are exceptions to every rule, and you'll see a number of them winning handsome checks on the tour. When one part of the body begins to move ahead of the other parts, however, it is extremely difficult for most golfers, myself included, to achieve the ideal clubhead path/clubface "geometry" at the start of the swing—that being, let me remind you once more, identical to the action of a swinging door.

Particularly when the hands and wrists get into the act too quickly, both clubhead path and clubface alignment are likely to become distorted.

The clubhead is swung either to the outside or inside of its ideal path, and perhaps also upward too quickly. Frequently, the clubface is also opened or closed relative to both the actual swing path and the ideal swing path. Then, because in most players the swing is an involuntary chain reaction, these initial distortions become magnified as the action progresses, forcing either mid-swing corrections or bad shots.

For those reasons, my goal when trying to play a straight, full golf shot with normal flight is to put every part of me in motion all together.

In actuality, as these photos prove, the first element to move in my swing is the head of the golf club, which gets going fractionally before my hands and arms begin to swing the handle. Nevertheless, the feeling I have in getting off to a good start is essentially a sense of "oneness"; of turning club, hands, arms, shoulders—my entire upper half—almost immediately clockwise as a single unit around the fixed axis of my spine in exactly the same way a door swings around its hinges.

I should probably note here that it wasn't always quite that way.

Until 1980, my primary feeling as I initiated the swing was of pushing the club straight back from the ball with a downward movement of the left shoulder and a consequent raising of the right shoulder, while simultaneously extending my arms as far away from my body as possible. This pattern came from my desire for an upright swing plane and the widest possible swing arc, and was encouraged at address by inclining my upper body well over the ball and setting my head well behind it.

As I described in the introduction, to this book, in order to "deepen" my swing in 1980 I had to stand more erect at address with my head more centered, thereby promoting a flatter shoulder turn. At the same time, I had to virtually reverse my theories on arm extension in order to make my arms follow the flatter shoulder turn and thereby end up deeper—i.e., less above and more behind me. Not surprisingly, these changes produced a different pattern of initial swing motion.

I might be able to convey a better picture of this new start-back pattern if I describe what I actually *see* as I begin the swing.

Because of my cocked chin, I have always been able to watch the clubhead move away from the ball in the peripheral vision of my right eye for about the first three feet of the backswing.

With the old swing, I wanted to see the clubhead travel directly back from the ball along a rearward extension of the target line for at least a foot before my gradually increasing upper-body turn moved the clubhead to the inside. Seeking then as now to keep the face of the club squarely aligned to its swing path—our opening-door analogy yet again—I also wanted to see little if any opening of the clubface relative to the target line for those first 12 inches or so.

Today I want to see a very different configuration.

As I start the club back with an "all-together" clockwise turning or coiling motion of my entire upper body functioning as a single unit, I want to see the clubhead begin to swing inside the target line almost immediately, then keep on moving progressively more in that direction as it swings out of vision. At the same time, I want to see the face of the club opening quickly relative to the target line and continuing to open as it disappears—indicating, of course, that it is remaining square to the arc of my now more sharply inward swing path.

To achieve those goals, it is imperative that my upper left arm remain close to my chest and that my right elbow start to fold almost immediately as the club begins to move, then stays close to my right side at least until my hands reach hip height. As I said earlier, this is almost an exact reversal of my previous concept of the correct arm swing, but it is imperative to achieving greater depth at the completion of the backswing.

If I can get these "geometrical" factors right as I start the club away from the ball, they will generally remain correct right on through to the top of the backswing and thus, reflexively, also through impact.

I think you'll find the same will happen in your game. And I think you'll get this "geometry" right most easily—plus insure a sound swing plane and a full body turn—by starting back from the ball with your entire superstructure and the club swinging into action as a single cohesive unit around the fixed axis of your spine.

See photos next page.

For me, getting the swing off to a good start means having a feeling of oneness—the club, hands, arms and shoulders turning almost immediately clockwise as a single unit around the axis of my spine. The clubhead swings naturally inside the target line and the clubface gradually opens in relation to that line, thus keeping the face square to my swing arc throughout the backswing and into the forward swing. Starting back with the entire upper half of my body insures a sound swing plane and a full body turn, which usually insures a good shot. When the hands and wrists get into the act too quickly, both clubhead path and clubface alignment are likely to become distorted. Therefore, I like to put every part of me in motion all together.

Four reasons for starting slowly

I believe that the pace of a person's golf swing is largely determined by personality. The quicker you do everything else in life, the quicker you will swing a golf club. And, of course, vice versa.

That being the case, I count myself fortunate in possessing a basically deliberate personality, because for me starting the swing slowly is absolutely vital to striking the ball truly.

I've said this many times before, but I want to stress it again here: I believe it is impossible to set the golf club in motion too slowly so long as it is *swung* rather than *taken* away from the ball.

There are four reasons why.

First and foremost, the slower the club is started back consistent with a smooth swinging motion, the more control the golfer has over the initial path of the clubhead and the alignment of the clubface. As we have seen, this is the only segment of the swing that most players can hope to fully direct mentally. Foul up here and, unless you have phenomenal reflexes, whatever mistakes you make surely will be reflected—and probably magnified—at impact. To me, it's just plain common sense that the faster you move the club away from the ball, the less control you have over its direction and attitude.

Reason No. 2 involves coordination. The more cohesively the various parts of the body go into action, the better the chance of making a correct and—note the emphasis—*complete* backswing. The faster most golfers start the swing, the harder it is for them to proportionately coordinate all of their bodily movements and to make a full upper-body turn.

Usually, when the initial motion is too fast or abrupt, the quick-acting smaller muscles of the hands and arms seize control, immediately outpacing the less-lively larger muscles of the shoulders, the hip mass and the legs. The various segments of the body then get more and more out of sync the farther the swing progresses, resulting in every imaginable kind of mis-hit plus, always, lousy distance. A sense of disjointedness during the swing, or an incomplete body turn, or a lift-and-chop, hands-and-arms-only swing, are always to me signs of too hasty or jerky a start.

Tempo and timing—maybe the least considered elements of the game among poor players—are my third reason for trying to start the swing as slowly as possible consistent with a smooth swinging motion.

The tempo and timing of the entire swing are *always* the product of its starting pace. The faster the overall swing, the less likely you are to get properly back before you start coming down, especially when the screws tighten. Very quick swingers historically have been streaky players—sometimes very good, but, when their timing was off, frequently very bad. Quick swingers also have generally been short swingers, and short swingers, historically, have mostly had short careers.

My fourth and final reason for an unhurried start is pressure. Everyone's actions speed up under any kind of pressure, an involuntary response to man's innate urge to fight or take flight whenever he's challenged. The slower and smoother your normal, unpressured swing pace, the more margin you have to accommodate the inevitable quickening when the heat is on.

As I said earlier, my swing has been timed at 1.9 seconds from take-away to impact. Of that time, about a full second is spent reaching the top of the swing. Even more time is spent changing directions at the top before beginning the forward swing and letting the clubhead speed build up gradually to its maximum. Starting back as slowly as possible while still swinging the club allows me to control the initial path of the clubhead and alignment of the clubface. It also lets me better coordinate the various parts of my body and make a correct and complete back-swing. In addition, it allows me to establish the correct timing and tempo for the entire swing and to have some margin to work with when my swing speeds up—as everyone's does—under pressure.

Chapter 6

To the top

Knowing the parts that make the whole

Like Sam Snead, on my very best days, given a good, smooth, slow start to the swing, I am not usually conscious of any particular elements of the remainder of the action. The club simply continues back and up, then comes down and through reflexively, leaving my mind free to focus exclusively on whatever type of shot I'm trying to hit.

This is a great feeling, but unfortunately such days are rare and never last very long in my case—any more, I suspect, than they do for other golfers. Somehow, it seems, we all eventually spoil these "it's-an-easy-game" spells by consciously or involuntarily overdoing or underdoing whatever was producing the magic. That's chiefly why no one ever seems to win more than six or seven tournaments a year of the 40 or more played annually on the American tour, and why probably no one ever will.

Not being a machine, you simply can't hold on to "perfect" form at golf for very long. The game is thus a continual balancing act, requiring endless swing adjustment and fine tuning. This, of course, despite the frustrations involved, is a big part of its challenge and appeal.

My knowledge of the many parts that go to make my whole swing was gained originally in learning golf. Since then it has been continually upgraded and polished in order to self-administer this balan-

cing and fine tuning. I use my knowledge first in thoroughly reviewing my fundamentals at the beginning of each year, always with the help of my lifelong teacher, Jack Grout. Then, during the season, as difficulties arise, I use it to solve them.

First, I do some quiet thinking away from the course about cause and effect. Second, I go to work on the practice tee on whatever specific elements of the swing I have by then reasoned need reviewing or revamping. I never have and never will beat balls randomly, which means hitting before thinking, and once I appear to have found a solution I quit. I want to save the good stuff for the golf course, not waste it on a driving range.

Also, I never conduct full-scale swing analyses or try to make big changes on the course itself. I learned a long time ago that when you are trying to score it's *always* better to make the best of whatever you have at the moment than risk compounding problems by attempting major surgery. The most I'll permit myself on the course are one or two key thoughts proven effective by past experience and directly related to the present condition of my swing. This often takes a lot of discipline, but then golf demands a lot of discipline at all times.

I outline these attitudes and systems in order to provide a setting for the way I henceforth intend to discuss the swing, and I hope it will guide others who might like to try my methods.

You have to learn the golf swing in your head and build it on the practice tee piece by piece, which requires studying and understanding it that

I like to keep my head quiet—not rigidly still—which allows my shoulders to turn more freely throughout my swing. My chin swivels away from the target at the start of the swing and then toward the target after impact.

way. When you take your swing to the golf course, however, it had better always be back together as a whole—be one single *flowing* entity. Try never to forget that, if the numbers on the scorecard are your top golfing priority.

Because the head is so critical to everything else, in dealing with the backswing I'll start with this element first and work downward. Then, because the through-swing must start from the ground up, when we change directions I'll begin with the feet and legs and work up.

Finally, I'll try to depict and describe my swing as the unified motion it must always be to work effectively as a competitive tool.

The role of the head

I've always believed that a very steady head is the bedrock of a good golf swing. It certainly has been critical for me, and it appears to have been a basic for almost all of golf's great champions.

When I wrote to this effect in *Golf Digest* several years back, however, Sam Snead suggested in an accompanying article that too much emphasis on restraining the head can restrict mobility in older and less-agile golfers. Better, he reasoned, to allow a little head movement if that's the only way you can swing fully and freely, than to freeze the head and thereby the entire action.

Sam makes a good point, which leads me to seek a better word than ``still'' or even ``steady'' for how the head ideally should behave throughout the swing. Maybe the word that best covers all bases is ``quiet.''

Some head movement is inevitable in every powerful full golf swing and in particular forms probably desirable. For instance, I swivel my chin away from the target at the start of the swing to make room for my shoulders to turn fully, then swivel it toward the target after impact in order to be able to watch the flight of the ball and make space for my right shoulder to turn through the shot. Also, photos indicate that my head moves slightly downward and backward during the downswing in reflexive response to my leg drive and unwinding of the hips—a move common to most good players.

Obviously, these are head movements, and I'm sure I'd be a lesser player without them. On the other hand, all three of these movements are both slight and ``quiet,'' and I'm even more sure I'd be a *much* lesser player if they became larger or ``louder.''

Why? Four reasons.

First and foremost, the head—or at least the top of the spine immediately beneath it—is the axis of the golf swing, the hub of a wheel-like rotation away from and back through the ball. Shift that axis up or down or from side to side and you shift the clubhead arc or path proportionately. The more you change the clubhead arc or path in mid-swing, the tougher it becomes to meet the ball solidly repetitively. In fact, many poor players need look no farther than ``noisy'' heads for many of their topped, thinned, fat and pop-fly shots.

Second is the much-neglected factor of balance. Proportionate to size, the head is the heaviest part of the body. Thus the farther you move it off center, as in swaying the upper body, the more you jeopardize your balance. When a golfer's balance goes, so does his swing.

My third reason for minimizing head movement involves torsion. The more fully you turn going back, the more torsion and leverage you create to be converted into centrifugal force then clubhead speed coming down and through. Fail to anchor the top of a coil-spring securely and it loses energy—you can't wind it as forcibly. Same with the golf swing.

Fourth and finally, the more the head moves the tougher it is to maintain sharp eye focus on the ball and the greater the risk of losing your sense of the correct target line and/or swing path. The better you watch what you want to hit and sense where you want to hit it, the better your chance of reaching your target.

How does a golfer learn to swing around a ``quiet'' head? Perseverance is vital, because very little in golf is harder to ingrain. The best head-steadying medicine Jack Grout ever gave me, because it keeps the body centered and teaches a sense of balance, is to practice hitting shots flat-footed, rolling the ankles but never lifting the heels.

If that fails, you could always try a method that Grout once used on me when desperate to implant in a stubborn kid the feel of swinging around a fixed axis. Simply have someone stand in front of you and hold tight to your hair as you swing.

You'll get the message—fast!

The upper body action

"You're not turning!" says a teacher or golfing pal. "Turn your shoulders fully," urge the books and magazines.

After "Keep your head still" and "Look at the ball," some sort of admonition to "turn" has to be the most common piece of advice in golf. Why, then, when it's been said so often—and is so obvious a *feature* in the swings of all good players— does it need repeating?

I think the answer is twofold. First, many golfers don't really understand the *objectives* of making a good backswing shoulder and hip turn. Second, even if they know why they should turn fully, many don't know *how* to do so. Let's see if we can clear up both problems here.

There are basically two reasons why fine golf is impossible without an adequate turning of the shoulders and hips in the backswing. One involves accuracy, the other distance.

Address a ball with any club and attempt to strike it hard without turning your shoulders *at all*. The only possible way is to swing the clubhead sharply up, down and up again, using your hands and wrists only, in an abrupt U-shape and in an almost vertical plane. Swinging thus, you'll be lucky to contact the back of the ball once in 10 attempts. Mostly, you'll top it or hit the ground behind it. The reason, of course, is that the arc the clubhead describes is way too steep to enable you to make clean contact with the rear of the ball.

Objective No. 1 of the shoulder turn, therefore, is to create a sufficiently wide and deep swing to enable the clubhead, in reciprocating the backswing arc coming down, to travel shallowly enough through impact to meet the ball squarely.

Essentially, the less you turn your shoulders and hips going back, the more you will be forced to swing only with your hands and arms. The more you use just those limbs alone, the more U-shaped and upright your clubhead arc must be and the smaller your chance of a square and solid strike. And, of course, the longer the club you are playing, the worse the problem becomes.

Now let's look at the distance factor. Repeat the no-shoulder-turn backswing and hold it there. Unless you possess Superman's wrists, I doubt that you could knock the ball much beyond the end of the tee. The reason is that you can generate almost no leverage or torsion with such an awkward and restricted action, and thus have given yourself almost nothing to convert into clubhead speed coming down.

Objective No. 2 of the shoulder turn, therefore, is to produce power —to generate clubhead speed through body leverage and torsion. There are limits to each individual's capabilities in this respect, which we'll discuss a little later. As a general principle, however, the more you turn your shoulders around a steady axis going back, the more leverage and torsion you will create. The more leverage and torsion you create, the more clubhead speed you will generate, thus—given also a square strike—the farther you will hit the ball.

I hope I've explained these basic "whys" of the body turn clearly, because understanding them is fundamental to building both precision and power in the golf swing.

Now let's look at the "hows."

The more a golfer inclines his upper body over the ball at address, the harder it is to rotate as opposed to tilting or rocking the shoulders throughout the backswing. I relearned this in 1980,

The first objective of the shoulder turn is to create a swing that is sufficiently wide and deep to enable the clubhead to travel shallowly enough through impact to meet the ball squarely and solidly.

in trying to develop a less upright and less U-shaped swing arc. Thus, if you have problems turning rather than tilting your shoulders, and a feeling of being ''in your own way'' as the backswing progresses, it's a sure sign of too much tilt. Try setting up to the ball more erectly. Keeping both your chin and your hands ''up'' at address will help you do that.

On tour there are a few super players who start the swing with the hands and wrists working the clubhead back well ahead of the rest of the body and still make a complete shoulder turn—Johnny Miller being a particularly fine example.

I think this is a tough maneuver for most golfers, for the following reason. The more the hands and arms swing the club back and up independently of the body, the quicker most players get a sense of having made a complete backswing. The sooner that feeling arrives, the sooner their shoulders stop turning.

The alternative is more of a one-piece motion of the entire upper body away from the ball, insuring that the shoulders and arms begin rotating *as soon as* the clubhead begins to move. Get your shoulders turning and your arms moving back along with them from the word go and their natural tendency will be to keep on doing so. Bring the shoulders into the act too late and—unless you're as athletic and talented as a Johnny Miller—they probably will turn too little.

Often in golf one brief, simple concept or thought—or even a single word—will help a player achieve a certain goal more than a year's tuition or a shelf full of textbooks. The thought that has probably most helped me insure a correct and complete shoulder turn over recent years is ''Swing around the axis,'' or, condensed to a single reminder word, simply ''Axis!''

This phrase or word triggers in my imagination a picture of a rod running through my entire upper body in place of my spine, which at address is positioned at a particular angle of inclination determined by the length of the club I'm playing. Thereafter, my goal is simply to rotate my upper body as fully and freely as possible around this axial rod *without changing its angle of inclination.*

If all else fails you in working for a full shoulder turn, try this swing-around-the-axis thought. In addition to whatever it does for your clubhead arc and clubhead speed, you will also find it an excellent deterrent against swaying and a fine way to insure a ''quiet'' head.

I like a one-piece motion of the entire upper body away from the ball, insuring that the shoulders and arms begin rotating as soon as the clubhead begins to move. Do this from the word go and their natural tendency will be to keep on doing so.

The arms

For 30 years, a very full extension of the arms away from the body on the backswing was fundamental to my game. I wanted an upright plane for accuracy and a big arc for power. Extending the arms first wide and then high assured me of both. Then, in the '70s, I fell unwittingly into a trap that lies in wait for all golfers by having gradually overdone a basically good move.

At address, the length of the club the golfer is using and his consequent distance from the ball preestablish the ideal plane of his arm swing. Ben Hogan illustrated this concept very graphically in his book *The Modern Fundamentals of Golf* by having artist Tony Ravielli draw an inclined sheet of glass reaching from the top of the ball up across Ben's shoulders, with a hole cut out for his head. The swath on the photo here depicts my ideal armswing plane with the driver in the same manner.

In early 1980, using this concept and with Jack Grout's help, I finally figured out why I could no longer achieve a full release and extension at the ball, or a sufficiently shallow-bottomed swing arc to strike it solidly. Increasingly for years I had been "breaking the glass" with every club in the bag. I had now carried extension to the point where, by over-separating my arms from my body, I was *lifting out of plane* on just about every backswing I made.

Over the years a lot of people have criticized what they chose to call my "flying right elbow." Well, they will be delighted to know that it finally did have to be modified. To lower or flatten my arm-swing plane—to keep it "under the glass" —required above anything else an earlier, easier and more downward folding of the right elbow in the early stages of the backswing.

Accepting all this emotionally wasn't too easy after three decades of total commitment to maximum arm extension as a fundamental of accurate and powerful golf. Resolving the problem physically was even harder, but it was finally achieved with the aid of three mental images, a new practice drill and a large amount of sweat.

Because "breaking the glass" is such a common problem among amateurs, I believe these images and the drill are worth passing on.

Years ago, when the stylish golf swing was somewhat flatter than it is today, teaching pros used to tell their pupils to keep a handkerchief tucked in their right armpit throughout the swing. While I didn't go to quite that length, I found it helped me fold the right elbow faster during the early part of the backswing if I imagined holding a small object between my upper right arm and right side—with a two-shot penalty if I dropped it before the club was at least halfway back. If these two parts of your anatomy stay close together, it's pretty darned difficult to make *any* kind of a backswing without folding and tucking the right elbow from the word go.

To lower or deepen my arms, I knew I had to tie their plane more closely to the plane of my flatter shoulder turn (to remind you, my shoulder turn was flattened chiefly by standing more erect and centered at the ball). I found the best way to achieve this was to try to maintain as constant a relationship as possible between the *top* of the club's shaft and the center of the body during the first half of the backswing.

Let me try to explain this a little more clearly.

You will find that, at address, the handle of the club points more or less to your navel. The longer you can keep it pointing there as you start back, the more "tied together" your arm swing and shoulder turn will be. The quicker the top of the shaft points away from your navel as the backswing progresses, the more you are "separating" the arms from the shoulders.

One great difficulty encountered by many golfers who've ingrained a lifting motion of the arms early in the backswing is making the hands swing the club sufficiently inward (rather than upward) starting back. I encouraged myself to start the hands more to the inside by erecting an imaginary curved wall along the outer extremity of the desired initial path. When that alone didn't do the trick, I covered the interior of the wall in my mind's eye with broken glass and razor blades, then imagined what would happen to my hands if they continued to misbehave!

Each of these visualizations helped ease my way along the rocky road to faster elbow folding, a deeper arm swing and a flatter shoulder turn. The most useful device of all, however, was a practice drill born of yet another piece of mental picturemaking. Imagining one day that my upper arms were literally strapped tight to the sides of my

See photo next page.

chest, I struck the ball so well that from then on I have employed that concept regularly in working on my game.

Using a short- or medium-iron, I try to make as full a swing as possible while keeping my upper right arm hugged tight to my right side on the backswing, and my upper left arm equally snug to my left side on the through-swing.

I probably never will fold my right elbow as quickly or as much as I should, nor get quite as deep with my arms as I would like, but this practice drill at least keeps me headed in the right direction. Also, it's a fantastic way of making the clubhead really work—and, equally important, of truly *feeling* it do so. I'll talk more about that later when discussing clubhead release.

Finally, one last correction to my previous ideas about the arm swing. There was a time when I thought the world would come to an end if my left arm did not remain perfectly straight throughout the backswing. That, again, went with maximum extension, and, of course, eventually contributed to an over-upright swing.

Today, as you can see in the photos, I've learned that as a fellow gets older and still seeks a full backswing he may need to "give" a little. The discovery has both eased the stress on my body and improved my clubhead release, and I wish now I'd made it a lot sooner.

A lot of people in the past have criticized my "flying right elbow," and they would be delighted to know that it finally did have to be modified. I no longer allow my arms to overseparate from my body or "lift out of plane."

The hand and wrist action

I learned to play golf—as you should also try to do—primarily with my strongest assets. In my case, these are the legs and torso. The result was that if everything else worked properly, my hands and wrists involuntarily did their job just fine. That's still pretty much the case today.

In swinging back, the chief job of my hands—and particularly the left hand—is to hang onto the club lightly but firmly, thereby insuring that it remains properly positioned relative to my arm swing and body turn. Some golfers have been able to play extremely well with a certain amount of slippage and/or regripping of the club during the backswing. To me, this makes an already complex set of actions even more complicated and I avoid it like the plague.

My wrists have really only one task during the backswing, which is to insure maximum leverage and proper positioning of the clubface and clubshaft at the top (more on those factors later) by hinging *reflexively* in response to the swinging momentum of the clubhead.

For 30 years I rarely found it necessary to give any of the above more than a passing thought. Today, I have become a good deal more conscious of hand and wrist action because of the swing changes I made in 1980.

As a result of standing more erect and centered at address and folding the right elbow sooner to promote a flatter shoulder turn and deeper arm swing, I sensed that my wrists needed to hinge or cock a little earlier going back than I would have thought ideal in previous years. When I went along with this inclination, I found it produced a commensurately earlier unhinging of the wrists coming down, making it much easier for me to achieve full release and extension at the ball. You might find the same thing to be true.

There have been a couple of other benefits, too.

In the old days, I suspect I sometimes delayed the wrist-cock too long going back in an effort to insure maximum arm extension and the widest possible swing arc. Since 1980 I've worried a great deal less about width of arc than depth of plane. As a result, I've found the slightly earlier wrist hing-

Although I cock my wrists earlier than I used to, they still begin to hinge relatively late in the backswing because I still believe that this action should happen in natural response to the swinging momentum of the clubhead. That means this hinging won't begin until the clubhead has climbed higher than the hands in the backswing.

ing to be excellent protection against extending my arms too far from my body during the early stages of the backswing.

If you're a "separator," you again might find a slightly earlier and freer cocking of the wrists helps you better meld the arm swing to the body turn.

The other benefit I've derived from the slightly earlier hinging involves the path of the club. Starting the club back immediately to the inside and keeping it going sufficiently in that direction to achieve adequate depth at the top has been my toughest challenge since the early '70s. The slightly earlier cocking makes this easier for me to achieve.

Now, having said all this, I should probably emphasize that these changes have only *marginally* altered my backswing hand and wrist action. My wrists still begin to hinge relatively late because I still believe that, at best, this action should happen simply in natural response to the swinging momentum of the clubhead. That means it won't begin until the clubhead has climbed higher than the hands in the backswing.

In my case, consciously manipulating the hands and wrists at any point in the backswing is a sure way to shift the clubhead out of its proper path, and also to foul up its face alignment relative to its path.

I think most other golfers will find the same thing. However, let me here once again repeat a piece of advice I've offered before in this book.

If something different works *consistently* well for you, then don't even consider changing. There are a lot of different ways to play good golf, and as long as you can put the good numbers on the scorecard, I promise you that no one will care how you do it.

The lower body action

Hold any pliable object—a soda pop straw would do fine—securely at one end and twist the other end. When you let go with the twisting hand, the object immediately springs back to its original form. That's torsion at work, and torsion, along with leverage, is the main source of golfing power.

The only way I know to pack sufficient torsion and leverage into a golf swing to reach all those long par 4s in two shots is to create some spring-like tension between the upper and lower halves of the body, and that will be our main subject here. But first, if I may, for those who genuinely would like to play better golf whatever the effort involved, a little honest fact-facing.

Quite often you will encounter a player with excellent mechanics—sometimes even a real picture-book swing—who hits the ball much shorter than you expect him to. Almost always the missing ingredient is torsion and/or leverage.

If such a golfer were an automobile, you might say that the bodywork was strong but the engine weak. And here's why the engine is so weak so often in recreational golfers. To create a lot of torsion and leverage takes strength and elasticity, muscular flexibility and dexterity—in short, good physical conditioning. That may be a sour thought to chew on, but it's the truth. If you sit in an office and an armchair all week and ride around the course all weekend, you are never going to pack much whack in your golf swing.

End of homily. Now on with the action.

To remind you once again, the chief role of the lower body in the backswing is to provide a stable base for, and a controlled degree of resistance to, what is going on up above. For that to happen, the upper body during this phase of the swing must *always* be the leader and the lower body *always* the follower. In other words, whatever moves occur from the waist down must be *in reaction to*, never the cause of, the actions taking place above the waist. If you get nothing else from this chapter, please lock that one single point permanently into your golfing consciousness.

Now, before I describe how my lower body works on a full swing, a word of warning. The less supple or athletic you are, the more movement you should permit through the hips on down in response to the turning of the upper body. This may cost you some resistance, and thus lose you a little torsion and clubhead speed, but that will be a lot less damaging to your scores than the overly U-shaped swing arc that will certainly result from an insufficient turning of the upper body through too much resistance in the lower half.

In short, don't restrict and steepen your swing arc by trying for more torsion and leverage than you are physically capable of achieving, because that will cost you accuracy as well as distance.

Here's how the lower body "chain reaction" feels to me during a full backswing:

As my upper half turns beneath my "quiet" head around the imaginary rod representing my fixed swing axis, the first response down below is a commensurate but *lesser* turning of the hips. I neither consciously restrain nor rotate my hips, but simply allow them to be *pulled* around naturally by the turning motion of my shoulders and the swinging motion of my arms. In doing so, I also want my hips, these days, to remain as *level* as possible at all times—no tilting, as in the old action. More on that later.

Because I am solidly built through the center section and make a very full shoulder turn, at the completion of the backswing with the longest clubs my hips have turned more fully than would those of a player with a more supple build or who turned his shoulders less. That's immaterial. What is important for all golfers, in terms of generating torsion and leverage, is that the shoulders always *out-turn* the hips.

As my hip turn continues in response to the pull of the shoulder turn and arm swing, so my legs and feet respond to the pull of the hips.

First, my left knee bends forward and then is pulled progressively more and more inward until, at the completion of the backswing, it has been drawn well behind a line extending vertically up from the ball. To enable that to happen without the hips and shoulders tilting or dipping, my left ankle also rolls progressively inward while the left heel gradually rises. Finally, with the woods and longest irons, the left heel is pulled clear of the ground as the backswing nears completion.

A natural reaction of this from-top-to-bottom coiling and pulling action is a gradual transfer of weight onto my right leg. The vital role of that leg is to serve as a brace to insure that my swing stays

The role of my right leg is to serve as a brace to insure that my swing stays "centered"—that it starts and continues to revolve around a fixed axis—while also "containing" the torsion that I am creating between my upper and lower halves.

The moves of the lower body should always be in reaction to the moves of the upper body. I neither restrain nor rotate my hips, but simply allow them to be pulled around naturally by the turning motion of my shoulders and the swinging motion of my arms.

"centered"—that it starts and continues to revolve around a fixed axis—while also "containing" the ever-increasing amount of torsion that I am creating between my upper and lower halves.

The right leg does this best when it takes the weight and resists the growing pressure of the bodily turning motion *with minimal change in its slightly flexed address position*. In actual fact, I make such a full turn with the longer clubs that my right knee slightly increases its flex and moves fractionally farther away from the target as the backswing is completed. Those movements are small enough to be tolerable in terms of permitting freedom of motion. If they were significantly larger, they would both dissipate torsion and change the clubhead path and arc I had established early at address.

It's a long time since I've had occasion to analyze an element of my swing as specifically as this, and if I tried to do so while playing I doubt I could break 80. Keep that in mind in working on your game.

By far the most important point about the action of the lower body as the club swings back is that, if your top half functions correctly, your bottom half will do all the right things *reactively*. That should always be your ultimate goal.

Two important angles

Let me remind you once again that the basic objective of the golf swing is to deliver the clubhead to the ball at the split second of impact traveling directly along the target line with its face looking squarely at the target. Two angles at the top of the backswing provide fine indicators of how well you are likely to achieve both of those goals if your downswing—as it should to play the game the most simply—basically reciprocates your backswing.

You can't see these angles yourself while swinging for real, but you can easily have them checked by a teaching professional, or even by a golfing pal with a knowledgeable eye. If you watch the pros on the practice tee at tournaments, you will often see them performing this small service for each other.

Let's look first at the clubhead path indicator. To explain it as clearly as possible, I've included three small diagrams (see page 97). Refer to these as you read what follows.

For the sake of this exercise, we'll assume you always swing the club back to a point where its shaft is horizontal at the top (not a bad goal, incidentally, with the longer clubs).

If at this point the shaft is also *parallel* to your target line, you can be sure that the path of your swing has remained constant and correct relative to the target line throughout the backswing (see drawing A). So long as your downswing action is then basically reciprocal, your clubhead path will have remained constant and correct through impact. When that happens, the clubhead approaches the ball from the inside, travels directly along the target line as it makes contact, then swings proportionately to the inside again on the follow-through. If the clubface also looks squarely at the target as it meets the ball, you can't fail to hit the shot dead straight to the target.

Troubles arise when the club at the top "crosses the line" (shaft pointing right of target; or is "laid off" (shaft pointing left of target). Then, as depicted in the two lower drawings, a downswing path reciprocating the backswing path must deliver the clubhead at impact *across* rather than directly along the target line.

When the shaft "crosses the line" at the top, as

In the ideal square position at the top, the back of the left hand, the left arm and the clubface are all aligned, maintaining the same straight-line relationship they had at address.

See Jack Nicklaus every month in GOLF DIGEST

Jack Nicklaus, Golf Digest's Chief Playing Editor, brings you his personal instruction series in every issue. Follow along with Jack as he shows you the mechanics and strategies he uses in his own game.

Improve your game with lessons from Tom Watson, Hal Sutton and other top touring pros who write exclusively for Golf Digest.

Bob Toski and the rest of the teaching professionals of the Golf Digest Schools will coach you in all aspects of the game.

You'll get all of the best step-by-step instruction as well as tournament news, reports on equipment, golf resorts and much more. Just fill out the coupon below and mail it today!

LOWEST PRICE AVAILABLE ANYWHERE!

No Postage
Necessary
If Mailed
In The
United States

BUSINESS REPLY MAIL
First Class   Permit No. 28   Harlan, Iowa

POSTAGE WILL BE PAID BY ADDRESSEE

GOLF
DIGEST

P.O. Box 3102
Harlan, Iowa 51593-2036

ldldll||lll||ld|lll||||||lll||lll||ll|

in drawing B, the reciprocal downswing path delivers it to the ball too much from the inside and then out beyond the target line. This causes either a pushed or hooked shot, depending on the alignment of the clubface. When the shaft is "laid off" at the top, as in drawing C, a reciprocal downswing sends the clubhead into the ball from the outside of the target line back across it. That produces either a pulled or sliced shot, again depending on clubface alignment.

In principle, then, the more nearly your clubshaft parallels your target line at the completion of the backswing, the better your chance of hitting the ball straight to your target. However, don't let yourself try so hard to be "perfectly parallel" that you destroy either freedom of motion or a shot pattern that allows you to score effectively.

As you can see in the overhead photo of me here, with my new swing I cross the line a little at the top with the driver as the result of a very full and flatter shoulder turn—in fact, one that has gone beyond the theoretical ideal of 90 degrees. This has promoted a draw rather than a fade as my bread-and-butter shot, and in recent years I've chosen to go along with it—not least because of the extra distance it gives me. You, too, might be happy with a right-to-left drift on your shots if it is

repeatable and controllable—and especially if you lack distance. However, I still believe completing the backswing with the shaft parallel to the target line is a good goal.

Conversely, if you lay the club off a little at the top but can still score reasonably well with the resulting left-to-right shots, think twice before you risk attempting major changes. Getting to parallel or slightly beyond at the top would make many recreational golfers better players by forcing a bigger body turn and a deeper arm swing, thus generating greater clubhead speed and a more-solid hit. On the other hand, doing so might take more time and effort than many of them are willing or are able to put into the game.

Now for the clubface alignment indicator. A while back I used the analogy of an opening door to illustrate the ideal relationship of clubface alignment to clubhead path during the backswing. You'll remember that as the door swings open its outer edge, representing the clubface, remains at 90 degrees—or exactly square—to the arc it is describing, representing the clubhead path.

The alignment of the back of your left hand relative to your left forearm at the top of the backswing tells you whether you have reproduced this ideal square relationship, and, if not, how not.

Assuming you set up correctly at address with the entire left arm and clubshaft forming a straight line from shoulder to ball, the back of your left hand and forearm must also be directly in line with each other as you start the swing.

When you arrive at the top with the left hand and forearm still so aligned, you have maintained the ideal door-like square relationship between the face of the club and the path of the swing. All other elements being correct, most golfers from this position will arrive squarely at the ball simply by swinging down reactively.

Troubles arise when a player changes the straight-line address relationship between the back of the left hand and forearm at some point in the backswing, generally by manipulating the hands independently of the body action. Then, one of two things happens, both of them—at least for less-skilled golfers—usually bad.

Most commonly, the left wrist cups or breaks inward, opening the clubface relative to the swing path. Short of a downswing correction, this leaves the clubface open at impact, causing a pushed shot or a push-slice. Alternatively, the left wrist arches or bends outward, closing the clubface at the top relative to the swing path. If the clubface then remains closed at the bottom—and this is particularly hard to avoid for most golfers—the shot is either a pull or a pull hook.

Quite a number of fine players over the years have been able to square the clubface by impact from a cupped-wrist, open-clubface position at the top by releasing early and rolling the hands and forearms through the ball. Because of the lively clubhead use this promotes, they have frequently been big hitters. Generally, however, such golfers have scored their best only when their timing was perfect.

Offsetting an arched-wrist, closed-clubface position at the top of the swing requires a very forceful driving of the legs and unwinding of the hips to delay the releasing of the clubhead with the hands and wrists coming down. Only a handful of players in my time on the tour—Lee Trevino being one of the supreme examples—has been able to handle these moves and stay at or near the top for a long spell. Generally, this type of action requires great strength and tons of practice—and even then distance and timing seem to remain constant battles.

Throughout my career, I have played my best from a square position at the top, have generally been able to at least get around the course in decent fashion from a slightly open position, but have almost always been a basket case when I have got the clubface closed.

I think most golfers will experience pretty much the same thing.

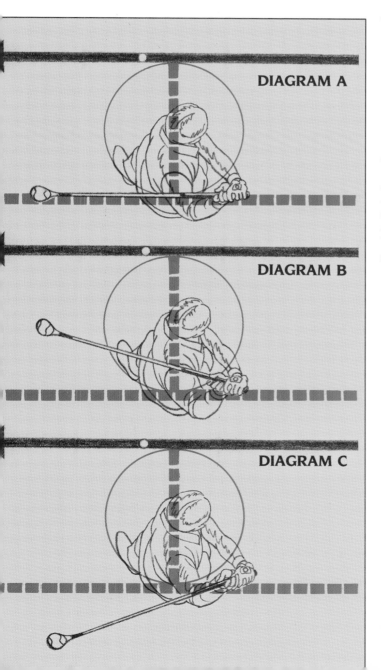

DIAGRAM A

DIAGRAM B

DIAGRAM C

The illustration at left shows the one right and two wrongs that can happen at the top of your swing. We'll assume in all cases that the shoulders have turned 90 degrees from the address position and the clubshaft is horizontal. In A, the shaft is pointing down a line parallel to the target line, which means that the club, your hands and arms are in good position for the return to the ball. In B, the shaft is "across the line," which will encourage a hook or push. In C, the shaft is "laid off," which likely will result in a slice or pull. Notice that all these shaft positions are in relation to the shoulder line. As long as the shaft remains perpendicular to the shoulder line at the top of the swing, it will be a good position. In the picture on the opposite page, my clubshaft appears to be across the line, but that is merely because I am turning my shoulders more than 90 degrees. The shaft is still perpendicular to my shoulders, so I'm in good shape.

No stop at the top

"Top of the backswing" is a convenient term and one that's probably been around ever since a Dutchman or a Scotsman first started thinking about how to hit a golf ball better. In actual fact, however, most good golfers never really achieve such a position. Neither should you, if doing so involves stopping moving in one direction and starting from cold in another.

High-speed photography shows that in the swings of almost all good players the clubhead is still moving back as the lower body begins to move forward. Ideally and most often this final backward motion is the product of a slightly increased hinging or cocking of the wrists. It is at best very slight, and always momentary and reactive, but it is present in every fine player who does not come to a complete stop at the summit of the swing.

You won't find many modern champions who have stopped completely at the top, and here's why:

First, a little extra wrist hinging as the swing changes direction is a sure sign of maximum backswing coiling—of high-octane fueling. Second, this slightly increased wrist-hinging is a strong defense against over-early use of the wrists and hands in the forward swing —the more they are cocked as they start down, the tougher it is to "throw" the clubhead with them too quickly. Third and most important, this additional hinging as the direction changes is proof positive that a golfer has stopped swinging from his upper half down and is now swinging *from the ground up.*

You can see this final backswing motion quite clearly in the photos of me here.

As my left heel is pulled by my body coiling to its highest point above ground in the first picture, indicating the completion of the backswing motion, the shaft of the club is just fractionally above horizontal. In the second photo the heel has started back to Mother Earth, indicating the start of the forward swing, but the shaft now is slightly *below* horizontal. Only in the third picture, with the left foot firmly replanted, does the shaft regain the slightly above-horizontal position it occupied as I "completed" the backswing.

You'll change swing directions most fluidly if you allow something similar to happen in your swing.

3

This mini-sequence shows that some part of me is continually in motion during the change from backswing to forward swing. In photo No. 1, my lower body has completed its turn while the driver is still going back. In No.2 my lower body has started forward while the club is still going back, and in No. 3 my legs are well into the forward move while the club has just started down.

Chapter 7

Down and through

Putting the forward-swing actions in perspective

Periodically over the years I've been asked to pose for photos in a top-of-the-backswing position. Usually I have suggested an alternative. The reason is that such pictures can never show the real thing.

In a moment I'll try to describe the actions of the forward swing in specific terms. Before doing so, however, I think it would be helpful to review how a fine golf swing actually works in totality.

Reduced to its bare bones, the full golf swing is simply a set of chain reactions. Here's how they work in all good players:

In preparing for every shot, the skilled golfer takes great care at address to establish through his grip, clubface alignment, body aim and posture the impact "geometry" necessary to achieve the desired ball flight. Initiating the backswing, he seeks a pattern and pace of motion that will preserve the correct geometry right on through to its completion, while allowing him to "fuel the engine" by coiling his body away from the target from his top half progressively downward.

At some point, depending on the player's physique and coordinative powers, he can coil no farther—can add no more fuel—without losing control, without destroying the geometry. At that point, he *instinctively* reverses the backswing process by uncoiling his body *reactively* back toward

the target from his bottom half upward.

When the player gets all this right, he returns at impact to a close approximation of his address position by *reflex*, which takes care of the geometry, which in turn gives him solid contact and accuracy. The backswing fueling, now converted into clubhead speed by the forward swing unwinding, takes care of the distance.

If all golfers were to set about learning and building a golf swing this way and *only* this way, I'm certain handicaps would be a lot lower.

However, probably because the forward swing is the part of the action that involves actually hitting the ball, most golfers can't resist analyzing it element by element. A good many also can't resist working on it while practicing and playing.

So long as you remember two hard facts, analyzing and consciously working on forward-swing mechanics may do you no harm, and perhaps even some good. Those hard facts:

In the long haul your forward swing will only be as good as your backswing. In turn, your backswing will only be as good as your preswing preparation. Thus, if you have a major fault in your forward swing, 99 times out of 100 you will permanently cure it only by identifying and curing the fault in your backswing. This again, 99 percent of the time, will involve curing one or more basic faults in your preswing preparation.

I hope as we now get into the mechanics of the forward swing that the preceding words will encourage you to view them in their proper perspective.

Remember, *please*, that every move I describe in this chapter works best when it happens as an effect, rather than as a cause.

The forward swing is an instinctive reversal of the backswing, the body uncoiling reactively from the bottom half progressively upward.

1

3

2

What actually happens from the top

As I've stressed so often in this book, my forward swing, properly executed, happens reactively in response to my preswing preparation and backswing. For that reason, it's not easy for me to describe in mechanical terms.

However, there is a need here to try to paint some kind of sensory picture of what actually takes place from top to impact and beyond. I believe I might best achieve that by focusing on one simple word. The word is "pull."

At the completion of the backswing, my left heel has been pulled well clear of the ground on the longer shots, and on the shorter ones I'm pulled at least onto the inner edge of my left foot. In either case, my initial move starting down is to firmly replant the left heel, I hope in exactly the same position it occupied at address.

The immediate result of this aggressive replant-ing of the left foot is a chain reaction, which I'll now try to describe as though I were consciously feeling each move in super-slow motion.

As I replant the left heel, it pulls my left knee back toward the target, which pulls my right knee in toward the target, which pulls my hips around toward the target, which pull my torso, which pulls my shoulders, which pull my arms, which pull my hands, which pull the club-shaft, which pulls the clubhead.

These are the sensations and the sequence of motions I believe I would experience if I could perform *the first half* of the downswing slowly enough to feel precisely what was happening, and in what order. As the action progressed farther into the downswing, however, and particularly since my 1980 swing modifications, the feelings would change. Here's how.

Originating always from the ground up, the chain-reaction pulling motion I've just described rises higher and higher through my body as it grows progressively stronger and stronger. In doing so, it creates an ever-increasing amount of centrifugal force in the head of the club.

Centrifugal force is the power that pulls an ob-

The first move starting down is the replanting of the left heel, which starts a chain reaction upward through the body—it pulls the left knee toward the target, which pulls the right knee toward the target, which pulls the hips around and in turn the torso, shoulders, arms, hands and club.

ject outward from its center of rotation. As the centrifugal force in the clubhead increases, it at first gradually and then ever more rapidly reverses the forces being exerted on my hands and wrists. Whereas they began to get into the act simply by pulling down on the shaft of the club in response to all the other pulling motion going on below, now the hands and wrists must increasingly respond to the pulling power of the centrifugal force acting on the clubhead.

The stronger this centrifugal pull, the more my wrists must unhinge. But, for that to happen, the less my hands and arms can continue to pull the shaft toward the target. This causes the hands and arms as a unit to eventually slow down their motion toward the target in direct proportion to the increasing speed of the clubhead.

As the hands and arms slow down, so the pulling toward the target of the body must also diminish to keep the two in step. Eventually, as the wrists unhinge completely in delivering the clubhead to the ball, the body ceases its targetward pulling almost entirely in order to let the hands and clubhead catch up with it completely and to become a firm brace for the hit.

Finally, as the hands totally release the clubhead through the ball and the clubhead begins to rise, it becomes the *new* pulling force, drawing the body completely around toward the target and the arms high above the head into a free and full follow-through.

Now, will any of the above help you build a better golf game? As an overall "sensory picture" of what the forward swing should feel like, *coming off proper preswing preparation and a sound backswing*, it can certainly do no harm.

What might help you even more—if you noticed it —is the absence of any mention of *positions* in this attempt to mechanically analyze a basically reflective set of actions.

Positions are paramount in golf in setting up to every shot, and they remain important right on through to the top of the backswing. Beyond that forget them.

You can't swing *to* positions coming down, only *through* them—and by then, anyway, the fate of the shot is sealed.

So go ahead and *hit* the ball with the head of the club, thinking—if you need to think of anything—about *motion*, not about mechanics.

As the hands release the clubhead through impact, the swinging force of the club then begins to do the pulling, drawing the hands, arms and finally the body toward the target, sweeping the hands high above the head into a full, free follow-through.

8

Striking a balance between body and hand action

From time to time I'll run across a player who prepares well at address and makes a good backswing, then wrecks shot after shot with a faulty forward swing.

Such golfers are usually pretty good at the game, which also indicates they are pretty studious about it. Frequently, I suspect, it's the studiousness that gets them in trouble by promoting either over-experimentation or over-emphasis on some seemingly "key" action.

As this book so emphatically illustrates, golf *is* a continual learning process. However, playing it consistently well, once you've ingrained certain fairly simple fundamentals, requires most of all that you avoid excess— maintaining a balance. The more analytical you are, the harder this can become, and particularly in the part of the swing that actually hits the ball.

Here's how to avoid the two most common forward-swing pitfalls—both of which, I might add, I've personally experienced at various times!

For about half of my professional career I played with such an upright arm swing that I was forced to use a great deal of targetward leg drive and hip unwinding coming down simply to be able to deliver the club along the target line, rather than from out to in across it. Although this happened reactively, it quite naturally promoted a strong mental awareness of those lower-body actions—to the point, in fact, where I stressed them heavily in clinics and writings.

When I deepened my arm swing and shoulder turn in 1980, at first there was no way I could release the clubhead quickly and fully enough to strike the ball solidly. Eventually it dawned on me that my new upper body action and my old lower body action were out of sync.

By continuing to work my legs and hips so aggressively, I was pulling my upper body too far around toward the target before I had time to fully release the clubhead into the ball with my wrists and hands. By decreasing my forward-swing leg-drive and hip-unwind, and making one other change we'll examine in a moment, I once again

As these three pictures show, the hands and arms and upper and lower body must work in harmony so that all parts of the body are in balance and in place at impact, no part outracing another.

became able to zap the ball right in the meat.

For most of its history, golf was played with the emphasis on hand action. In modern times, the emphasis has switched to leg and body action. The truth is, to strike a golf ball hard and true you need to use *every* part of your body in *balanced proportion*.

If on the forward swing your legs and body get ahead of your wrists and hands—which can easily happen if you consciously force their action—the clubhead will arrive at the ball too late, costing you distance by meeting the ball too steeply or obliquely, and direction by leaving the face open.

Conversely, if you under-work your lower half relative to your wrist and hand release, you'll hit the ball fat by delivering the club too shallowly and miss the target because you've closed its face too quickly.

Beware, then, of over-emphasizing any particular action just because it happens to have become a point of emphasis among analysts and theoreticians.

Know your own swing, know cause and effect, stick with fundamentals, and strive always to keep everything in *balance*.

What "over the top" really means—and why it happens

Like all sports, golf has its own lingo. One example you'll frequently hear if you mix with good players or listen to the analysts on tournament telecasts, is "over the top"—as in "The ball's in the boondocks because he came over the top on that swing."

What exactly is a golfer *doing* when he makes this obviously undesirable move, and what are the results? I suspect many players aren't quite as clear about that as they would like—and need—to be. Let's try to resolve the mystery.

In a nutshell, a golfer swings "over the top" when, for whatever reason, *his arms and right shoulder move closer to the target line coming down than they were going back.*

You can see this move most plainly by standing behind a right and then a wrong golfer looking through them down their target lines.

In the correct golfer, the shoulders in the first part of the forward-swing stay turned away from the target line enough for the arms to swing the club *down* either along or a little inside the plane of their upward swing. Watch the hands in relation to the right shoulder to get the sharpest impression of this. The more they separate—the quicker a gap appears between the hands and the right shoulder and then widens—the better the forward-swing form.

Now for the over-the-topper.

As this golfer swings forward, his shoulders begin turning towards the target immediately. This forces his arms to remain high and to swing *around* rather than down past his body, so that when eventually they do descend they are on a plane *outside* the plane of their upward swing. Watch the hands in relation to the right shoulder again and you will see that, compared to the good golfer's, the two separate much more slowly and sluggishly. That's proof positive of swinging "over the top."

When it is pronounced this move usually feels ugly and inhibiting to the player, and it certainly looks that way to all knowledgeable observers. It also has three very ugly effects on a golf ball, as follows.

First, the over-the-top swing delivers the clubhead from out to in across the target line, which produces a pull or slice depending on where the face looks. Second, it delivers the clubhead too steeply, sometimes resulting in a topped shot, sometimes in a fat or heavy hit, sometimes when the ball is teed in a blooper. Third, if you make this move habitually it will inhibit full release of the clubhead, thereby diminishing speed and distance.

From what I've seen in pro-ams, I would estimate that about 90 per cent of amateurs swing over the top to some degree on about 90 percent of their full shots. Why, when the results are so punishing, do these golfers repeat themselves so persistently?

The answer at this level of the game lies almost entirely in improper pre-swing preparations and faulty backswings.

As the great scientist, Sir Isaac Newton, said so long ago, "Action and reaction are equal and opposite." Swinging over the top for the higher handicapper is mostly an irresistible involuntary reaction to a bad grip, or lousy aim and alignment, or incorrect posture, or all three, leading to a poorly-shaped and energy-deficient backswing.

However, even very good golfers come "over the top" on occasion, especially when they are nervous or "tight." Generally the movement is slight compared to the high handicapper's, but, in a game of fractions of inches, the effects can be just as devastating on the scorecard. What's the reason in the good player's case?

If a golfer's mechanics are sound through the completion of the backswing, I look first at the quality of his clubhead release into and through the ball. Very often the problem lies simply in "hanging on" to the club too hard and too long with the hands and wrists—in trying to steer the ball with the body rather than hit it with the weight at the end of the stick.

This becomes particularly prevalent when, for whatever reason, a golfer loses confidence in his swing, or is under extreme competitive pressure, or both. Frequently then the tendency is to become over-conscious of swing "position" or ball destination, or both, at the expense of *clubhead motion*. In short, the golfer tries to "place" the ball where he wants it with his body, rather than slinging it there with the head of the golf club.

If you would like to prove or reaffirm to yourself how insufficient wrist and hand release forces you over the top, try the following experiment.

Pick up a club and make a normal backswing, then, as you get to the top, grab the shaft tightly enough to lock your wrists and forearms. Now, with your forearms and wrists locked, try to make your regular forward swing.

You will find that your body turns back towards the target pretty much as normal. What you will also find is that your arms, instead of swinging down and under, now are forced to swing *out and around*, with the club staying high in the air. The harder you clamp your hands and lock your wrists, the higher and more out and over your shoulders and arms and the club will swing as you turn your body back toward the target.

Experimenting like this, of course, produces an exaggeratedly over-the-top motion, but on a lesser scale this is exactly what happens when an otherwise good golfer hangs onto the club too long. It may be a super way to hit something above ground, like a sinker in baseball or a low return in tennis, but it's an awfully difficult way to try to hit a golf ball solidly in the rear.

Thankfully, at least for better players, the problem is usually easily solved, and I'll offer some thoughts on that later.

To avoid coming over the top, the shoulders should stay turned in the first part of the forward swing long enough for the arms and hands to swing down inside—or at least along—the path they took on the backswing. A good indication of a correct swing is, as you see here, that a gap appears quickly between the hands and the right shoulder as I start down and widens considerably into impact, while the arms and the right shoulder never move closer to the target line than they were going back. This means that the hands and arms are swinging independently of the shoulders and are bringing the clubhead into the ball on a path from inside the target line.

Five aids to a complete release

Despite the fact that, thanks to Jack Grout, a full use of the clubhead has been one of my fundamentals since childhood, I discovered that I was hanging onto the club too long soon after I began to revamp my swing in early 1980. The problem started out as a physical one, then became compounded psychologically, which is the typical pattern with most golfing faults.

As I've explained a number of times, it had become physically impossible for me to release fully through impact due to my over-upright armswing. Much as I tried, there was always a little bit of involuntary "blocking" through impact with the wrists and hands, simply because my body wasn't in a position at that point to let everything go freely.

Even when I solved that swing plane problem, actually achieving an early enough release to meet the back of the ball solidly was for a time the very devil of a job. Back I would go deeper with my arms and shoulders then out and around they would come in the classic over-the-top action before I could get the clubhead to the ball.

The reason, of course, was that the long-ingrained physical block had now produced a mental block. I was still swinging "scared" in my head, which made it just about impossible for my wrists and hands to behave as they should.

An internal pep-talk ultimately resolved much of the psychological block. Hot and frustrated one day, I decided to let it all hang out and to heck with where the ball went. "You're not having fun with what you're doing," I told myself, "and above all golf is supposed to be fun. As a kid you let it all fly then went and found it, and golf was always fun in those days. Either do that again or quit."

This sort of attitude at least got me mentally prepared to use the weight at the end of the stick as aggressively as possible, which helped a lot in freeing the muscles. The finishing touches came over the next few weeks with the help of two swing thoughts or concepts, plus three specific practice drills.

Conceivably, one or more of these would help other golfers with the same sort of problems.

Thinking of using the weight on the end of the club aggressively helps free the muscles and promotes a full and effective release through impact, eliminating any tendency to "block" the rotation of the arms and the unhinging of the wrists—just let it fly and go find it.

The image of "restoring the radius"—returning the left arm and clubshaft to the same position at impact they were in at address— aids a full release.

1. Think "restore the radius"

The first and probably the most important swing image I worked with in 1980 to improve my release was a mental picture of "restoring the radius" at impact in order to achieve full extension at the ball.

In setting-up for a normal full shot, you will notice that most good players' left arms and club shafts form an extended straight line from the left shoulder to the ball with pretty much every club in the bag except the putter. This establishes a certain radius of swing determined by the length of the club. If the golfer's hands did not then hinge at the wrist, or his left arm bend at any point in his swing, this radius would remain constant both away from and back to the ball. The arc the clubhead describes would then, of course, be a true circle, and full extension at impact would be achieved automatically.

Man, however, isn't built in such a way that he can generate high speed in the head of a golf club without hinging his wrists. Whether they do so early or late, a lot or a little, to strike a golf ball effectively the hands *must* hinge at the wrists in the backswing then unhinge in the downswing.

So, yet again, the game confronts us with a piece of "geometry."

As the wrists hinge going back so, obviously, the radius of the clubhead's arc progressively decreases. To achieve solid impact we must then, coming down, progressively reverse this process by unhinging the wrists until, at the ball, the address radius is fully restored again.

The surest indicator of whether or not a golfer is restoring his radius is his degree of left arm/clubshaft extension through impact. He has perfectly restored the radius when his left arm and clubshaft again form an extended straight line as he strikes the ball.

When the shaft lags behind the arm, the hit is "late" because the unhinging—the *release* in golfing terms—has been insufficient. Conversely, when the left arm lags behind the clubshaft through impact, the hit is "early" because the wrists have unhinged— *released*—prematurely.

The thought of "restoring the radius" helped me greatly back in 1980 in a number of ways.

Because over-tilting or dipping the shoulders and hips during the swing obviously decreases the radius established at address, this piece of imagery first of all encouraged me to stand "up" to the ball at address, then maintain my height in my head, shoulders and hips, which helped produce a flatter backswing turn and a deeper arm-swing. Next, it suggested a less aggressive forward-swing leg-drive and hip unwinding, allowing more time for my hands and wrists to keep pace with my body. Above all, it promoted the liveliest possible use of the weight on the end of the stick right from the top of the backswing.

I've always believed that, given proper pre-shot preparation and a sound backswing, it is impossible to release the club too freely and fully with the wrists and hands so long as you begin to move onto your left side as soon as you start down to the ball.

By thinking "restore the radius for full extension at the ball," I finally got to doing that again.

2. Hold your shoulders until last

When I talked about swinging "over the top," we saw that if in starting down your arms and right shoulder move over and around closer to the target line, rather than down and under your head on the same plane as they swung back, you will hit lousy golf shots.

Chiefly because of a poor set-up and/or improper lower-body action, the less-skilled golfer's first move in changing directions is a spinning motion of the upper body. Sensing that this over-the-top action must deliver the clubhead too steeply and from out to in, he then instinctively holds back on it, either by grabbing harder with the hands, or spinning the shoulders even more, or falling away from the target in the classic "fire and fall back" action.

In short, this golfer doesn't release fully because he is anatomically incapable of releasing fully—his initial forward-swing body action forces his arms

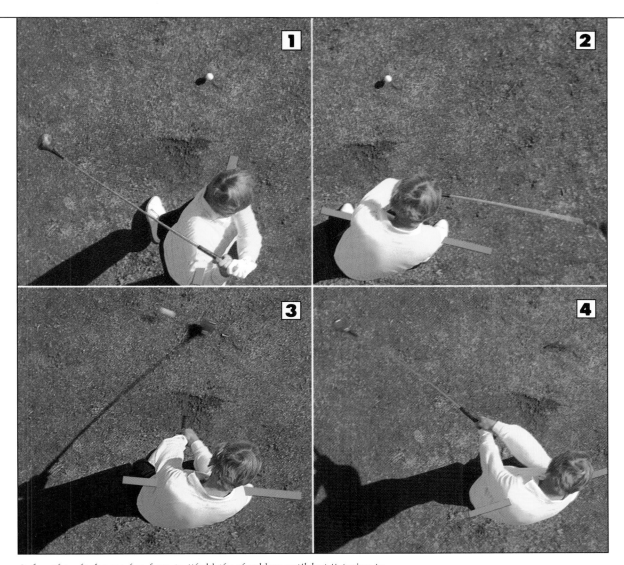

A key thought for me has been to "hold the shoulders until last," trying to keep the shoulders in the top-of-the-backswing position as long as possible while the forward swing unwinds from the feet up. I imagine an unbendable steel rod running through my shoulders and I try to feel on every shot that I get the clubhead to and through impact before that rod and my shoulders turn past parallel to the target line. Note in the fourth frame here that even after I have swung well into my follow-through, my shoulders are turned only slightly past that parallel position. Keeping the rod turning last as your arms swing down will go a long way toward giving you an effective, on-line release. If you are a chronic over-the-topper, doing this might at first require almost forcibly holding back your shoulders.

and hands too far out of position to allow him to do so, even when he consciously tries.

I think many such players might get some help from the second of the swing images I used back in 1980 in working on clubhead release, and periodically still do in practice. It's pretty simple but, if your pre-swing preparation is sound and you make a passable backswing turn, it also can be pretty effective. Once again it involves thinking "geometry" as well as motion.

In setting-up to every shot, you (I hope) carefully identify then strongly visualize your direct ball-to-target line—ideally to the point of actually "drawing" such a line in your mind's-eye. If you plan to hit the shot straight to the target, you then (again I hope) set your shoulders parallel to the target line in taking your address position.

For the purpose of this exercise, forget the target line once you have set your shoulders parallel to it. In its place, focus exclusively in your mind's-eye on an imaginary line running through your shoulders. Go to the point even of imagining a solid unbendable steel rod connecting your shoulders and protruding through the top of each arm.

As you swing back, try to consciously "feel" this rod turning along with your shoulders. At the completion of the backswing the rod should have turned through at least 90 degrees relative to its address alignment—maybe a little more.

Now comes the vital piece of imagery.

As you start down—beginning, of course, from your feet up—*try to keep the rod in its top-of-the-backswing alignment as long as you possibly can.*

If you are a chronic over-the-topper, doing this might at first require almost forcibly holding back your shoulders while your knees start towards the target, your hips start to unwind and your arms start to swing downward. Initially, it will probably be a pretty darn tough move to make. For that reason, I suggest you try it at first in slow motion and without attempting to actually hit balls. In fact, work on it initially away from the golf course so that you aren't tempted.

When you think you've gotten fairly comfortable with the move, go ahead and hit some teed balls using a medium iron and an easy swing. Try as you do so to sense the difference between your present sequence of forward-swing actions and your old sequence.

Starting down in the past, your shoulders would

have been the first part of your body to move forward, thereby *pushing* your arms, hips and legs towards the target. Now, as you hold the steel rod and your shoulders back until last, your legs will be *pulling* everything towards the target—first your hips, then your arms, and finally your shoulders and the rod.

Ingrain that pulling feeling, with the rod always unwinding last, and your arms swinging *down*, and you'll have come a long way to better ball-striking. To go the rest of the way, try using the shoulder rod imagery as I did in 1980 when I learned to release fully along a flatter arm plane.

Try for a feeling on every shot of getting the clubhead on the ball *before your shoulders turn past parallel to the target line.*

If you need an additional mind-picture to help you do that, imagine your shoulder-rod as a stick bomb that will explode if you ever let it point left of the target before a switch can be thrown. The switch-thrower is the clubface.

The switch, of course, is the ball!

3. Let your left heel rise

Achieving total release of the clubhead through the ball has been a primary goal of my full-swing practice sessions since early 1980. To promote it I regularly use one or more of three specific drills.

To explain the first of these requires visiting again our old friends Cause and Effect.

The less a golfer's left heel lifts going back, the more his left hip is forced to drop and his right hip to rise in response to the pulling of the arms and shoulders as they attempt to turn fully. The more the hips rock or tilt going back, the more they will rock or tilt the other way reactively swinging down. The more tilted the hips during the forward-swing, the less easily they can rotate targetward. The less easily the hips rotate targetward, the less room the golfer makes for his arms to swing freely past his body—the more, so to speak, he "gets in his own way."

The more in his own way a *good* golfer gets coming down, the harder and longer he involuntarily

Allowing the left heel to be pulled clear of the ground proportionate to the amount of shoulder turn enables the hips to rotate sufficiently so I "get out of my own way" and my arms can swing past my body. This lets me release my hands and arms fully and produce a full extension at impact.

hangs onto the club with his hands and wrists to prevent his upper body from spinning out and over. The longer and harder the good golfer hangs onto the club with his hands and wrists, the less freely he slings the clubhead into the ball.

Or, in a nutshell: heel down=tilting hips=blocked arms=restrained hands and wrists=short and crooked golf shots.

(Poor golfers may sometimes do just what I describe here. More commonly, however, they react to "getting in their own way" by collapsing the left arm, or falling back onto their right foot, or flipping the clubhead at the ball with a kind of weak scooping motion—or all three. The results are uniformly disastrous.)

The good golfer's chain-reaction just described had become a real bugaboo for me before I changed my swing in 1980, chiefly as a result of being too upright, but also partly because of not allowing sufficient heel lift with all but the longest clubs. Consequently, since the swing change I work periodically in practice on consciously allowing the left heel to be pulled clear of the ground going back proportionate to the amount of shoulder turn I am making.

By doing that I reduce the amount of tilting or rocking in my hips, which enables them to rotate sufficiently to make room for my arms to swing freely past my body, which allows me to release my wrists and hands fully, which produces full extension at impact.

If you feel "blocked" or "in your own way" during the later stages of the downswing, you might find a little more left heel lift mighty helpful.

4. Keep your right heel down

Way back when my main golfing goal was to squeeze every possible inch out of my driver, allowing my legs and hips to get too far ahead of my wrists and hands was a recurrent problem. The result was late application of the clubhead to the ball, thus an unrestored radius at impact, thus on many occasions a wild and woolly golf shot.

Eventually, Jack Grout laid down the law. "Young fella," he said one day, "for the next two weeks—or two months, if necessary—I don't want to see your right heel raise off the ground before the shot is in the air. Use your ankles but keep that right heel down on every swing, no matter what. That will be hard to do at first, but it will force you to use the clubhead to hit the ball, not your body."

If I remember correctly, this drill originally was conceived by that great old teacher, Alex Morrison. The effect when Grout laid it on me was so beneficial that I actually played for close to two years without coming up off the right heel until the ball was on its way.

If you choose to try this drill, do so at first using a short-iron with the ball teed high. Be sure to keep your right knee flexed through the top of the backswing, be equally sure to work your ankles during the forward swing, and be patient as you graduate to the longer clubs.

What you will find is that, as you hold your right heel down longer, your body will not unwind towards the target quite as quickly. This forces your arms to swing on a more *downward*—rather than a rotary—path, which encourages your wrists to unhinge faster, thereby applying the clubhead earlier.

I should mention that this particular drill has other benefits besides promoting a complete release.

When the right heel rises too quickly in the forward swing, the right knee is thrown forward, which pulls the right hip forward, which pulls the right shoulder out and around, which forces the left leg to stiffen, which forces the entire body to spin even more. When the right heel stays grounded longer, you'll find that, starting down, your knees are forced to shift directly towards the target, which keeps everything up above coming at the ball from well inside the target line.

In short, this heel-down drill is a great antidote for "over-the-toppers," as well as for non-releasers.

Jack Grout's advice to keep the right heel down helped me slow the movement of my legs and hips on the downswing, and let my hands and wrists keep pace. It's a drill that not only promotes a complete release, but also will help you eliminate coming "over the top" by holding the right knee, and therefore the right hip, in place longer.

5. Marry your left arm to your left side

My third practice drill for ensuring full use of the weight on the end of the stick represents a complete reversal of my pre-1980 ideas about the proper way to hit through a golf ball.

For most of my career, I regarded maximum targetwards extension of both arms beyond impact as proof positive of maximum forward-swing acceleration. Thus I tried to "chase" the ball with my arms as strenuously as possible. Not surprisingly, in that light, I also placed heavy emphasis on full arm extension after impact in books and magazine articles.

Well, today, the farther toward the target my arms extend after the ball has been hit, the more certain I am that I've failed to release the clubhead early enough!

Here's why.

As we saw earlier, the more upright a golfer swings his arms, the more aggressively he must drive his legs and hips toward the target starting down in order to be able to get the clubhead on the ball before it passes beyond the target line. The more violent these lower body actions, the stronger the pull on the golfer's arms. The stronger the pull on the arms, the more a golfer will sense that his clubhead speed is coming ultimately from *acceleration of the arms*, rather than from an unhinging at the wrists and a slinging action of the hands.

That was me to a T throughout most of the 1970's. Things began to change when, after deepening my backswing in early 1980, I found that my old aggressive leg-and-hip drive made me continually "late" with the clubhead. Gradually, I began to quieten the lower-body action. As I explained previously, the more I did so the less conscious I became of pulling arms as the final forward-swing accelerator and the more conscious I became of unhinging the wrists and slinging the hands. Ultimately, as my sensory perceptions steadily reversed, it dawned on me that, if the arms don't actually *slow down* some at some point in the forward-swing, then the wrists can never unhinge sufficiently to fully "restore the radius"—achieve maximum extension—at impact.

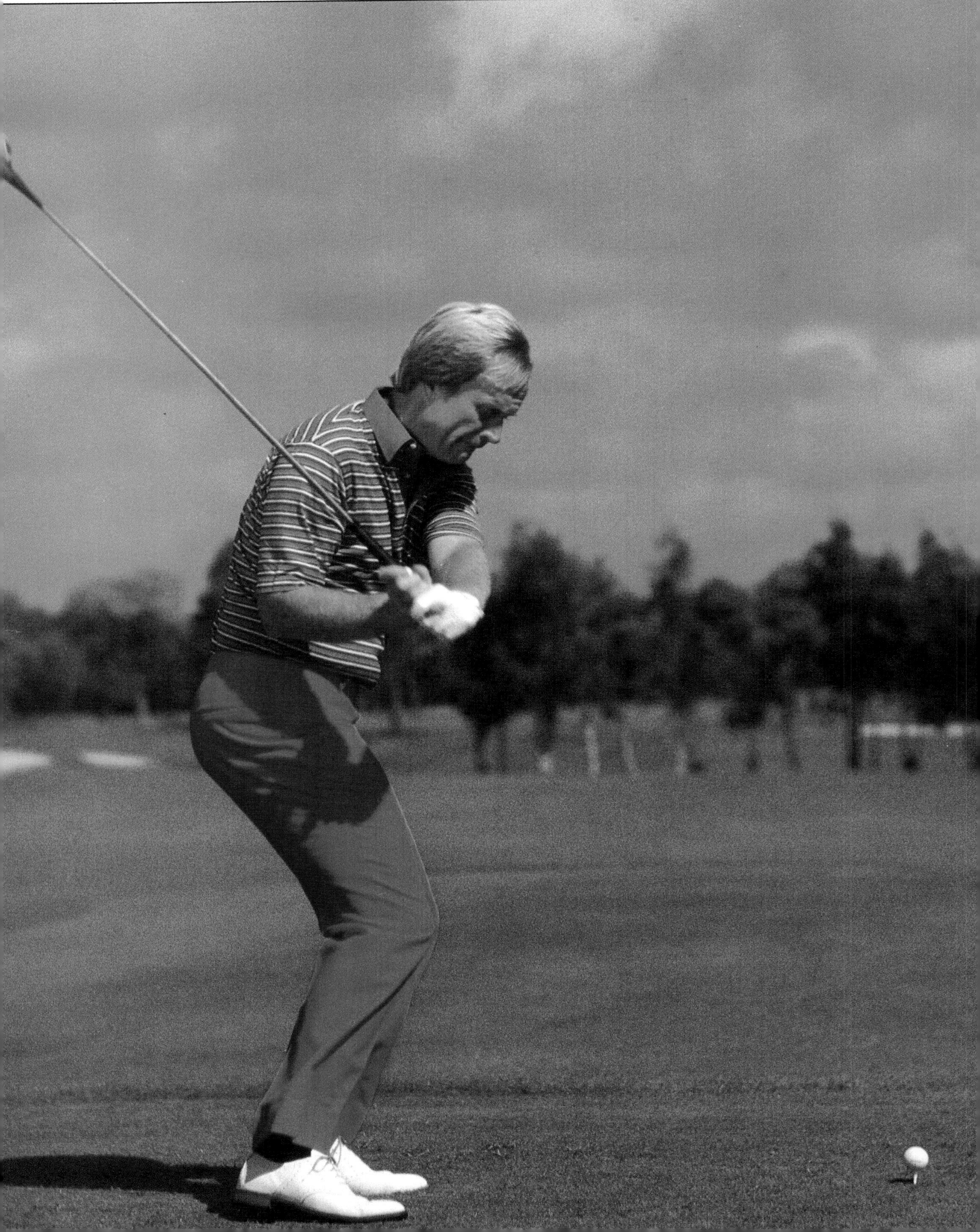

From this discovery, with the help of Jack Grout and Phil Rodgers, came the drill that I now use most regularly in working on a complete release. What it does, in essence, is to create rapid *reflexive* unhinging at the wrists at the appropriate point in the forward-swing by marrying the pace of the arms to the slower motion of the body as it unwinds towards the target.

Here's how I apply the drill in sensory terms.

As a result of my flatter arm and shoulder plane, at the completion of the backswing my upper left arm is now snug against the upper left side of my chest—no separation as in the old, over-upright days. Swinging down in the past, the more I extended the arms through the ball the more the left upper arm would have separated from the chest.

Swinging down now, I work to keep these two segments "married"—to keep my upper left arm tight and snug to the upper left side of my chest—from the completion of the backswing as deeply into the follow-through as the momentum

of the clubhead will allow.

In actuality, as the photo on page 120 shows, the two must eventually separate. They obviously will do so faster the longer the club being used, because of the greater momentum in the clubhead. Nevertheless, my *sensory* goal, in practice, is to keep the marriage intact as long as I possibly can without forcibly restricting my follow-through.

To sustain this marriage requires, in my case, a quicker folding of both elbows immediately after impact than in the old days, plus an earlier rolling of the right hand over the left. I find that neither is possible unless I begin to sling the clubhead towards the back of the ball with my wrists and hands right from the moment I have moved onto my left side starting down.

At its best, the forward-swing feeling this drill creates is that of a shallow or "low" clubhead arc moving into and through the ball, with the clubhead climbing quickly after impact as the product of a complete release. For too many years prior to

Another way to keep upper and lower body in sync during the downswing is to "marry" your left arm to your chest. I've eliminated the separation that used to be there in my swing, forcing a quicker rolling of right hand over left—and a more complete release.

1980 I had suffered exactly the opposite sensation—of the clubhead swinging steeply or from high up into the ball and then low for quite a way after impact. The present from low-to-high feeling certainly makes for much zippier and less effortful golf shots.

In addition to promoting maximum use of the clubhead, this drill has three other benefits. First, the clubhead swings inside the target line faster, with its toe turning skyward more quickly, indicating a through-swing arc reciprocating my flatter backswing, and thus complete squaring of the face at impact. Second, I finish the swing more erectly, or less in an inverted "C" position, with my entire body directly facing the target, indicating excellent balance and a lesser strain on my lower back.

Third and most importantly, the drill gives me the best sensation of completely releasing the clubhead and fully extending my left arm and the club shaft through the ball that I have yet discovered in 34 years of playing golf.

If you've never found or have lost that super sensation, give this drill a thorough try. It could make golf a whole different game.

The "marriage" drill gives me the feeling of a shallower clubhead arc, climbing quickly after impact for zippier, less effortful shots.

After the ball has gone

Scientists have determined that, when hit with the driver by a powerful golfer, the ball is in contact with the face of the club for about one two-thousandths of a second. They say it takes about ten one-thousandths of a second for the feel of impact to run up the shaft and through the player's hands and arms to his brain, then about a fifth of a second for a message to come back from the brain to the hands. By then the ball has traveled about 50 feet.

I give you these figures to indicate the futility of trying to do something to a golf ball with your follow-through. Once the club and ball have met, the shot is history. In terms of ball-control, therefore, what you do with the club after impact is immaterial.

In two other respects, however, the follow-through is far from immaterial. First, as the final effect of all you have caused to happen previously, it is a fine yardstick of your overall swing mechanics. Second, trying to achieve a particular form of follow-through in practice can help a basically sound golfer to attain other swing goals.

The best service the follow-through provides for me is a measurement of my balance during the swing. If I am properly balanced as I complete the swing, I can be pretty sure that I was properly balanced throughout the entire action. If my balance is improper on the follow-through, I know something has gone amiss earlier. I will then review each of my pre-swing and backswing fundamentals until I diagnose the problem, using the follow-through as the ultimate arbiter. You should do the same.

I also get help from the follow-through in checking the plane of my swing.

Ideally the plane of the follow-through should mirror the plane of the backswing. Unless you go to the trouble of filming or taping your swing, you can't see whether this is happening yourself, which is another reason why you need a competent teacher who knows your game intimately if you seek to play golf seriously.

Jack Grout will check this element of my swing frequently in our sessions together. If the two planes don't match, we then look for the cause. Almost always, we find it either in my aim and alignment at address or in my initiation of the backswing.

That's where your problems will almost certainly lie if the planes aren't pretty much reciprocal.

The fullness of the follow-through with the longer clubs is a fine measure of your clubhead release through the ball. The better your release, the greater the momentum in the clubhead, and the more momentum the clubhead carries, the farther up and around and then down behind you it will travel in the follow-through. If I don't finish a driver swing with the clubhead back down below my waist, I know I'm not releasing fully. Again, that puts me to work on reviewing previous elements of the action that can cause this effect.

The alignment of the body at the completion of the swing can also provide a good golfer with valuable information.

Ideally, at this point the body should directly face the target. If the body swings much past that position, chances are the player is coming "over the top," probably through insufficient targetward

leg-and-hip drive initiating the forward-swing. If the torso stops short of facing the target as the clubhead completes its journey, the golfer probably is "blocking" his arms, wrists, hands and the clubhead by overusing his lower body starting down—by sliding too far laterally instead of making a combined slide/unwind.

In practice I sometimes will build into my pre-shot preparation a mental and sensory picture of how the end of a perfect follow-through looks and feels. Then, when I swing, I will focus only on trying to be picture perfect. That's really putting the horse behind the cart—effect ahead of cause—but such imagery can sometimes be helpful if the pre-swing and backswing fundamentals are basically sound.

I also find this piece of imagery helpful in working on tempo and timing, because it forces me to become more conscious of the total flow of swing motion, and thus less concerned with the bits and

pieces that go to make the whole. Finally, it's a great way to overcome "ball fixation."

As has been said so many times, one of golf's greatest challenges is that the darned ball doesn't go anywhere until *you* move it. Among poorer players, this produces a tendency to *hit at* rather than *swing through* the ball. Perhaps because of the almost hypnotic effect that inert little object has at times, even the best golfers sometimes catch this disease, and it almost always has a fatal impact on the scorecard.

Pre-programming myself to achieve a certain pattern of follow-through has cured me of this on a number of occasions by decreasing my ball-consciousness—by making the ball something that simply will be incidentally swept away if I complete the swing correctly.

Conceivably, the same technique might do the same for you.

Though it's futile to try to do anything to the ball with your follow-through—it's too late by then—your finish is a yardstick by which to measure your swing mechanics. By aiming for a sound, balanced position at the finish you will naturally help groove the other elements of your swing.

Chapter 8

Mainly photos

The complete swing reassembled

If you possess an instinctive genius for golf, you may be able to play it very well without knowing much about its technique. Unfortunately, the game's history indicates that instinctive golfing genius is extremely rare.

For most people, becoming a consistently fine golfer requires sufficient effort and patience to acquire a thorough understanding of the various components of the swing, and of how each interrelates with all the others.

One difficulty in this process is that we are bound to analyze and study statically what only finally works as one continuously flowing motion. For the fact is that, no matter how well you learn the basic ''positions'' essential to a good action, the final key to playing well is learning to swing *through* them, never *to* them. In the end, therefore, controlled repetitive *motion* becomes much more important than detailed mechanics—and, to compound that problem, motion can only be learned by feel and never by reason.

In this book, like most others on playing golf, I've necessarily had to focus a lot on mechanics, although I've tried whenever possible to also describe the feelings and motions inherent in a good golf swing. Now, as we reassemble the swing in totality and look at it from four different angles, I suggest that you forget mechanics entirely, and try instead to imagine and imprint in your senses a feeling of the *overall motions* conveyed by these sequence pictures. To help in that, I've briefly noted under each photo my impressions of the motions I'm making or the muscular feelings I'm experiencing at the various points in the swing.

To encourage you in this, I'd like to repeat something I said back before starting to talk about the swing itself: ''Never make the mistake of trying to swing in a step-by-step or part-by-part manner. An effective golf swing is above all else a continuous *flow of motion*, and the less you need to direct or dissect it while actually playing the game, the better the motions will flow.''

The Motion: Swivelling the chin away from the target, a fine way to both trigger the swing and avoid starting from a ``frozen'' position.

The Motion: Everything swinging back together in a smooth, unhurried, well-coordinated one-piece start.

The Motion: *The wrists begin cocking involuntarily only in response to the clubhead's increasing momentum.*

The Motion: The spring coils to its fullest around a steady axis, totally ``gathering'' me for the change of direction.

The Motion: *Starting and continuing down from the bottom up—the feet go to work first, then the knees, then the hips.*

The Motion: The hands and wrists beginning to apply the clubhead, as the uncoiling lower half squares
              the shoulders to the target line.

The Motion: *The radius formed by the left arm and club at address fully restored, squaring the clubface solidly at impact.*

The Motion: *The clubhead freely tracking the ball, as the upper body remains well behind the point of impact.*

The Motion: The entire body releases, unwinding freely targetwards beneath the continually ''quiet'' head.

The Motion: The clubhead's momentum completes the swing with the body in perfect balance and the belt buckle facing the target.

The Motion: *Beginning smoothly, deliberately, "quietly" from a feeling of relaxed-but-ready springiness.*

The Motion: *The club swings on the correct inside plane purely in response to the one-piece coiling of the torso and arms.*

The Motion: *The left heel begins to rise as the coiling of the upper body pulls the left knee in towards the ball.*

The Motion: *Maximum coiling from feet to shoulders, signalling complete readiness to let everything fly reactively.*

The Motion: *Leading and pulling the shoulders and arms with the feet, knees and hips—the only way to keep the club swinging on the correct plane.*

The Motion: Now really slinging the weight at the end of the stick—fully releasing the clubhead with the hands and wrists.

The Motion: *The left side still commanding the swing, but now the right side is completely into the act also.*

The Motion: *Both arms extending fully targetwards, chasing the ball under a still ``quiet'' head as the body continues its rotational unwinding.*

The Motion: Freewheeling, as the clubhead momentum naturally pulls the right hand over the left and almost all the weight shifts to the left side.

The Motion: *Finding and watching the ball again as the action winds down with no sense of discomfort*
or loss of balance.

The Motion: As well as being a good trigger, swiveling the chin to the right also clears more space for a full, free body turn.

The Motion: *The upper body controlling the coiling, and still working as a one-piece unit, but with the left leg responding to its pull.*

The Motion: *The solidly planted right leg braces the action ever more firmly as the upper body turn and coil progresses.*

The Motion: Coiled or wound or turned as fully as the physique allows, short only of losing control over the body or the golf club.

The Motion: *Left foot solidly replanted first, with the right knee pushing and the hips rotating towards the target.*

The Motion: *The upper right side and arm still well behind or ``under'' the left until the hands and wrists have fully released the clubhead.*

The Motion: *Everything except the head and the hands and arms rotating smoothly towards the target as the clubhead meets the ball.*

The Motion: *The arms and hands begin naturally to follow the body rotation, allowing the clubhead once again to swing inside the line of flight.*

The Motion: *The weight shifting almost entirely to the left side as the clubhead's momentum and body rotation finally force the head around but never ``up.''*

The Motion: Weight on the outside of the left foot and lightly on the toes of the right, with the hands
            swinging all the way back behind the head.

The Motion: *Whatever your preferred "trigger," stay slightly in motion somewhere in your body until you're ready to pull it.*

The Motion: *The left shoulder begins turning from the moment the clubhead leaves the ball—the only way to achieve a properly wide and deep arc as well as a one-piece start.*

The Motion: The shoulders and hips coil in unison with the inward and upward swinging of the arms —neither element outpacing the other all the way to the top.

The Motion: *The shoulders always out-coil the hips, but the hips must turn around and back to get and keep the weight fully behind the ball.*

The Motion: *The right elbow drops and remains close to the side of the body as the lower half initiates and leads the downswing.*

The Motion: Everything moving at maximum speed as the hands and wrists release the clubhead—but still swinging around the fixed axis established at address.

The Motion: *The alignment of the shoulders at impact momentarily reproduces their alignment at address —square to the target line.*

The Motion: *The head and upper body remain behind the position of the ball until it's well on its way —the product of a full, free release of the clubhead with the hands, wrists and arms.*

The Motion: *The right hand climbs quickly over the left in a natural response to great clubhead momentum—another sign of a proper release.*

The Motion: *The head remains in the same place and plane as at address, simply rotating to look past*
the arms as the rest of the body completes its well-balanced unwinding.

Different clubs but the same swing

Many beginners at golf, if not quickly instructed otherwise, think they must learn a different swing with every club in the bag. If that were true, an already immensely difficult game would become virtually impossible. Thankfully, this is the exact opposite of the truth, and we run these sequences and the ones immediately following to prove the point.

Here you see me swinging a driver, a 2-iron, a 5-iron, an 8-iron and a pitching wedge. In every case the set-up and swing pattern are basically the same. Essentially, unless I am trying to create an abnormal flight, only three things change whenever I am hitting a golf ball through the air.

First, as the length of the shaft shortens, I am obliged to stand progressively closer to the ball. Second, the *scale* of the swing—the amount of body motion and the arc of the clubhead—decreases as shorter shafts and increased clubface lofts progressively change the emphasis from power to precision. Third, I progressively narrow my stance—by moving the right foot closer to the left—to accommodate my decreasing body motion and my increasing need for club control.

Please believe me, then—the secret to good shotmaking is not 14 different swings, but *one fundamentally sound swing.*

Plus, of course, a good putting stroke...but that's another book!

DRIVER

2-IRON

5-IRON

8-IRON

PITCHING WEDGE

DRIVER

2-IRON

5-IRON

8-IRON

PITCHING WEDGE

Flighting the ball

For the sake of clarity, I have talked throughout this book about the full swing in terms of hitting the ball dead straight. As I explained in chapter one when beginning to discuss targeting, very few of the best golfers attempt to do that. Generally, they either predominantly fade or draw their routine shots.

Top golfers also, of course, have the ability to curve the ball severely when special circumstances so demand, and, even more importantly, to vary its height. This book would, therefore, not be complete without a few pointers on these techniques.

There are at least three ways to curve the ball from left to right or from right to left. Jack Grout taught me what I believe to be the simplest during boyhood, and I have stuck with it ever since. Its basis is different sets of body and clubface alignments but a normal golf swing on every shot.

To start the ball left of target and then curve it right, I first identify my *direct* ball-to-target line by standing behind the ball looking through it to the target. Next, I decide how much left of that line I want the shot to start, then find a mark on the ground 15 or so feet ahead of the ball directly on the intended line of initial flight. In setting-up to the shot, I then align my shoulders, hips, knees and feet *parallel to this line of initial flight*, NOT to the true

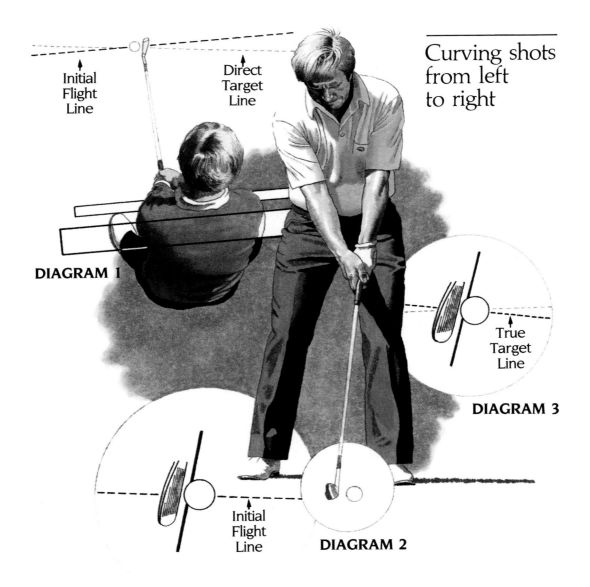

Initial Flight Line

Direct Target Line

Curving shots from left to right

DIAGRAM 1

True Target Line

DIAGRAM 3

Initial Flight Line

DIAGRAM 2

target line (see diagram #1). This takes care of the ball's starting direction.

Next, I build in the curvature by opening the clubface at address *relative to the line of initial flight*, not to the true target line. Also, and most importantly, I open the clubface without changing my grip—*without altering the alignment of my hands relative to my body* (see diagram #2).

If I want just a little fade, I will have aimed my body left only marginally, and thus will open the clubface only slightly. If I want a big slice, I will have aimed left a lot more and thus will also open the clubface a lot more—perhaps even to the point where the clubface now also becomes open to the *true* target line (see diagram #3).

Finally, once I am confident that these alignments are correct, I simply go ahead and make my normal golf swing, relying entirely on the inter-action of the preestablished clubhead path and clubface alignments at impact to produce the desired curvature.

To draw or hook the ball, I simply reverse the above process, aligning my body to the right and closing the clubface proportionally relative to the ball's initial starting path. Then once again I make my normal golf swing (see diagrams #4-6).

As I said a moment ago, there are other ways to curve a golf ball, and if you have found one that works for you, fine and dandy. If you're having trouble in "shaping" shots, try my way.

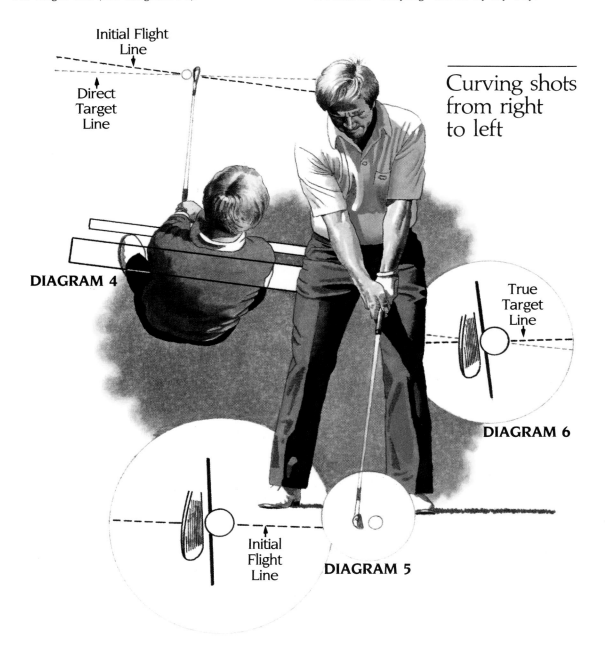

Initial Flight Line

Direct Target Line

DIAGRAM 4

Curving shots from right to left

True Target Line

DIAGRAM 6

Initial Flight Line

DIAGRAM 5

A golfer needs only two things to vary the height of his shots: an understanding of three basic principles, then the will to work with them assiduously in practice.

The first principle is that backspin produces height, thus the less backspin you impart to the ball the lower it will fly. The more you shorten the shaft of the golf club by choking down on its grip, the less backspin you'll generate, therefore the lower the trajectory of the shot with any given club.

The second principle is that the positioning of the ball relative to the feet allows you to change the effective loft on the face on the club. Move the ball back in your stance and, as long as you leave your hands in their accustomed address position, you deloft any given club and thus will automatically hit the ball lower with it. Conversely, move the ball forward while situating the hands normally and you increase the club's effective loft, thereby creating a higher trajectory.

The third and final principle involves clubface alignment. The more you close the clubface at address and impact, the further you deloft it and so the lower yet the ball will fly (but in this case, note, with a strong right-to-left or hooking flight). Con-

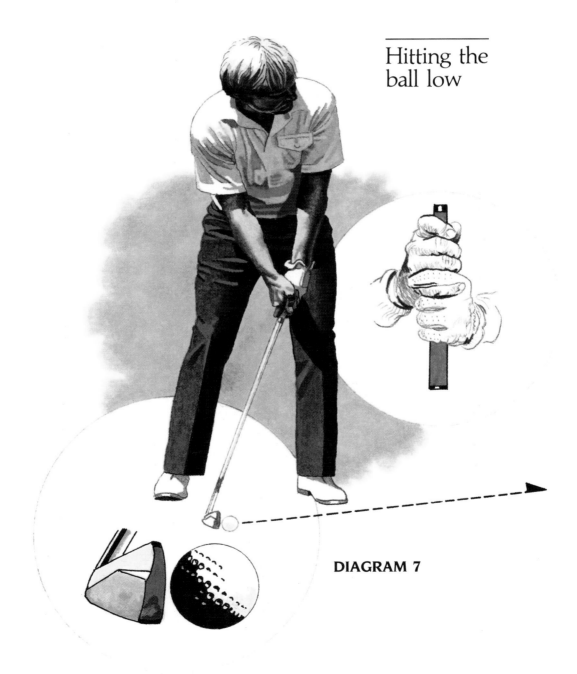

Hitting the ball low

DIAGRAM 7

versely, the more you open the clubface, the more you increase its effective loft and thus the higher the ball will fly (but with a pronounced left-to-right or slicing flight).

For the ultimately low shot, therefore, you would grip way down the shaft, move the ball far back in your stance, close the clubface as much as you dare, and allow for a considerable amount of hook and a great deal of run. Conversely, for the ultimately high shot you would use every bit of shaft available, play the ball well forward in your stance, open the clubface wide, and allow for a fair amount of slice and very little roll.

And in between these extremes? Unfortunately, this is a "finesse" element of the game that you can't be taught by books or even direct coaching, but must gradually learn for yourself by experiment, experience and practice.

Make the effort, because the ability to control the height of your shots is basic to your eventual scoring capability.

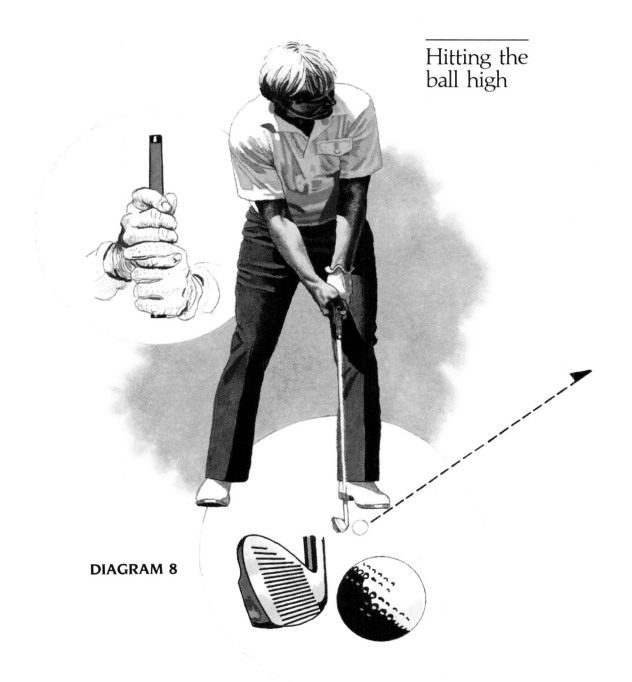

Hitting the ball high

DIAGRAM 8

Tempo and timing

In the same way that I try to use one swing for every club, I try to swing each club at the same basic tempo. The sequence photos indicate that I come pretty close.

All the sequence pictures of my swing in this book were shot with the same camera operating at 75 frames per second. On pages 166-169, we show ten sequence exposures of me swinging, from top to bottom, the driver, the 2-iron, the 5-iron, the 8-iron and the pitching wedge. Using the moment the clubhead leaves the ball as the starting point, each of these photos in the complete sequence is separated by the same number of frames. As you can see, I arrive at very nearly the identical points in the swing at the same time with all five clubs.

Because I am by nature a basically deliberate kind of guy and have a very full golf swing, my overall tempo is toward the slower end of the scale. I think this has contributed greatly to both my ability and longevity as a golfer. Consequently I would advise other players to try for at least an *unhurried* tempo.

Unfortunately, in many cases this can involve fighting a war with one's personality, because, if a fellow is quick and abrupt in all his other actions, he will tend instinctively to be quick and abrupt with a golf club in his hands. If that's the case, I think the best policy is usually to build a swing that works within your natural quick tempo, if only because it will become all but impossible to resist your instincts under pressure.

Whatever the pace or length of your swing, the one quality of motion you should always work for, in practice and play, is *fluidity*.

The less *flowing* your movements at every stage of your actions in every phase of the game, right from the moment you draw a club from the bag, the more foul balls you will hit. In that regard, try particularly to remember a point I made in chapter five when talking about starting the swing: *the mood of the initial motion establishes the mood of the entire motion.* In other words, start the swing jerkily or hurriedly and you will continue to swing jerkily or hurriedly.

Here are a few specifics that might help you stay smooth and fluid:

• Don't rush *anything* before you play an important round of golf. On tournament days, working back from my starting time, I give myself at least an hour to get ready for the world, and at least another hour to do all I have to do at the golf course, plus ample traveling time.

• In the golf swing you first accelerate the club (away from the ball), then decelerate it (at the completion of the backswing), then accelerate it again (down and through), then decelerate it (at the completion of the follow-through). The more "oily" you can make those transitions of pace—to borrow a marvelously descriptive word from Sam Snead—the better you will play.

• Swinging smoothly and fluidly becomes impossible when you grab the club tighter at some point in the action. You can insure against this by holding on very lightly in setting-up to the ball, then firming the hands to their firm-but-light pressure just before you begin the swing, then trying to maintain that pressure throughout the swing. If you're going to err in grip pressure, err on the light side.

• Think "I can't hit a golf ball with my backswing." Think "Get all the way back before you start down." Think "Complete the backswing!" Think all or any of those things, especially when you're playing poorly or the conditions are rough or the pressure is grabbing you by the throat.

• Try to maintain the tempo of your backswing into the first part of the forward swing—especially with your hands. You'll move everything faster involuntarily coming down, but trying to sustain your backswing tempo helps smooth out the change of direction. "Waiting for the clubhead" at the top also will help you do this. Try not to start down until you can feel the mass of the clubhead against the tension of the shaft.

• Hit balls on the practice tee with your feet together—actually touching at the heels and toes. If you aren't pretty darned smooth then, you will fall over.

• If you keep falling over, you might have to face the fact that your mechanics are so bad that it is *impossible* for you to swing smoothly and fluidly. In that case, I suggest you quit playing the golf course for a while and go get some lessons from a good teaching pro, because what you are doing to yourself out there can't possibly be much fun.

Ladies and lefties

In this book I've referred to the golfer as "he" not out of chauvinism but for convenience and clarity. Writing "he or she" every time may be desirable in our present society, but it also, unfortunately, makes for extremely cumbersome and pedantic prose. I've tried to put the message ahead of all other considerations, and I hope the ladies will understand and bear with me.

Obviously, this book is written from a male perspective. Nevertheless, scaled to the relative degrees of physical strength, I believe everything I have tried to pass on here about golf applies just as much to the female player as it does to the male. Should you want to prove that to yourself, just spend an hour or two sometime at an LPGA tournament!

In the same way and for the same reasons of clarity that I've stayed with one gender, I've stuck to playing golf from one side of the ball. Naturally, I chose my side—the right-handed side. There are, however, many thousands of left-handed golfers in the world— both male and female—and for them I felt that, even if we can't get the syntax right, we can at least provide some correct pictorial references.

On the following pages, therefore, the lefties will find what I believe to be the most important photos in this book flipped and reprinted. My suggestion is that, if a point isn't completely clear when read from a right-handed perspective, the left-hander refers to these pictures of me looking as he or she does.

I believe this is the first time such a thing has been done in a golf instruction book. I hope it helps a group of people much neglected by those who write about how to play this marvelous game.

An easier way to swing—Page **10**

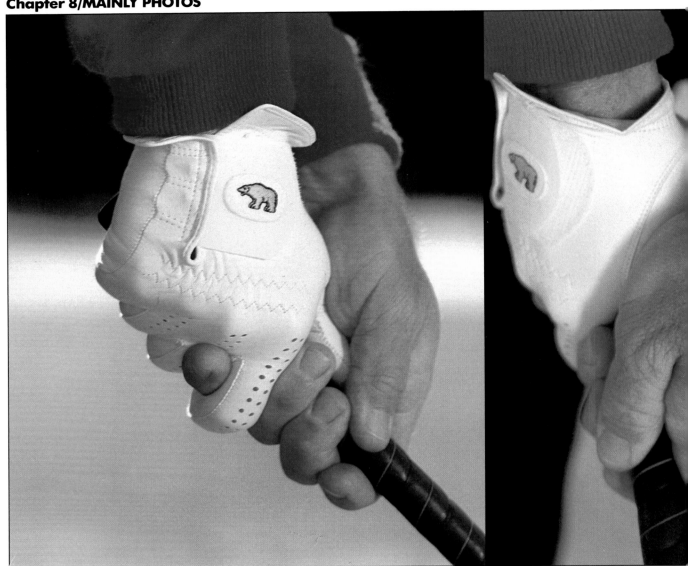

Your grip is the foundation of your golf swing
—Page **28**

"Marrying" your hands
—Page **37**

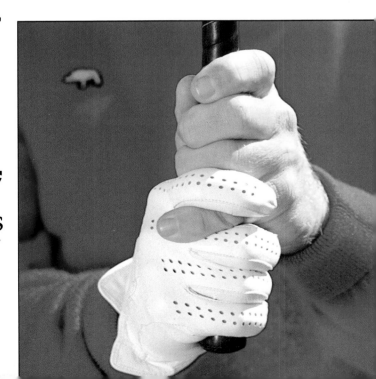

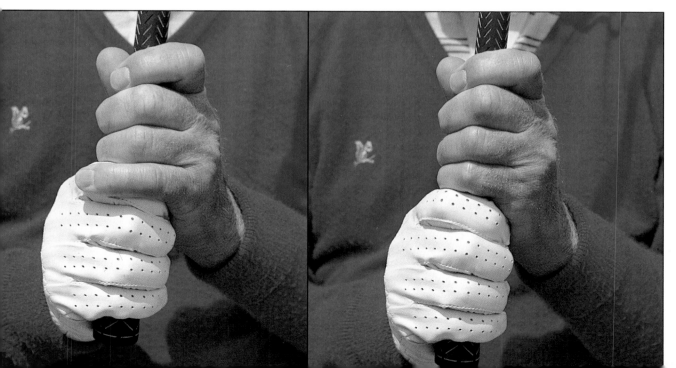

Approaching the ball
—Page **44**

Aiming your body
—Page **49**

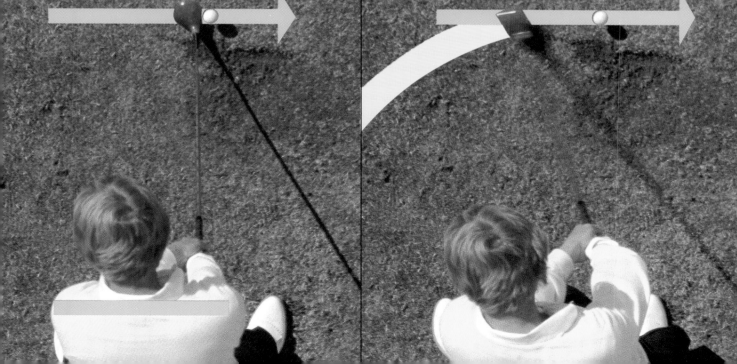

Ball positioning—a way to simplify the game
—Page **50**

Guaranteeing a descending blow
—Page **53**

Hitting the driver at the bottom of the arc
—Page **53**

Distancing yourself
from the ball
—Page **54**

Angling your feet
—Page **59**

Positioning your head
—Page **61**

Hang loose but lively
—Page **64**

Making the motions flow
—Page **71**

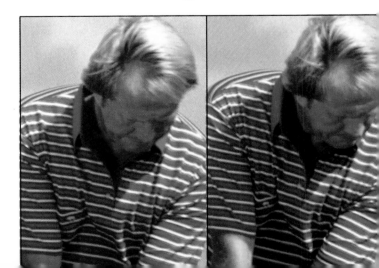

Clubhead path and clubface alignment
—Page **72**

Getting it going all together
—Page **74**

The role of the head
—Page **83**

The upper body action
—Page **84**

The lower body action
—Page **91**

The hand and wrist action
—Page **89**

No stop at the top
—Page **99**

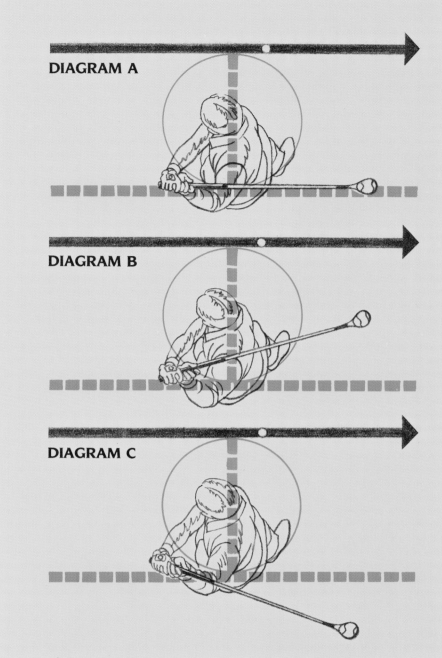

DIAGRAM A

DIAGRAM B

DIAGRAM C

3

Two important angles
—Page **94**

What actually happens from the top
—Page **103**

What "over the top" really means —and why it happens —Page **108**

Think "restore the radius" —Page **112**

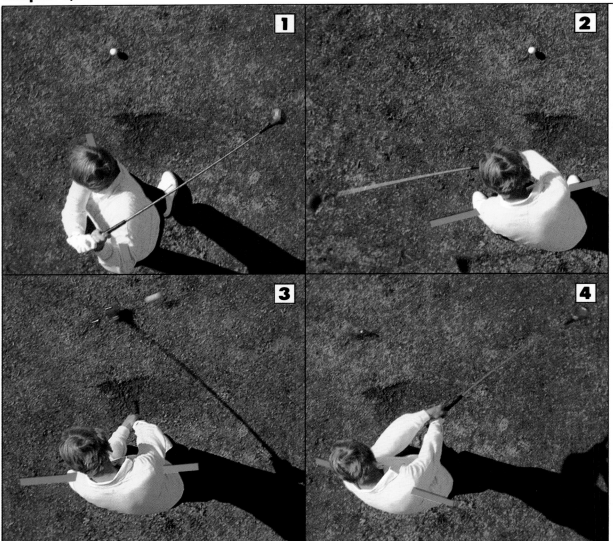

Hold your shoulders until last
—Page **112**

Let your right heel rise
—Page **114**

Marry your right arm
to your right side
—Page **117**

After the ball
has gone
—Page **121**

The lesson I'll never forget

I started playing golf for fun, and, of all the things the game has since come to mean to me, having fun is still by far the most important.

That's why, when the fun started to diminish at the end of the 1970's, I rebuilt first my short game and then my full golf swing. I love the healthfulness and beauty and camaraderie of golf, but for me in the final analysis the fun of the game grows proportionately to how well I play it.

As you've read this far I guess we have that in common, so I really do hope there is something in these pages that will help you play better.

The best thing that happened to me in both my original golf learning and my mid-life relearning processes was having a great friend and teacher in Jack Grout, and maybe that's something you would do well to ponder. I can't think of many top golfers of my generation who haven't had outstanding teachers.

Next, I would recommend that, however or from whomever you seek improvement, you stick to fundamentals, keep things as simple as possible, and try to build a swing that makes the most of your own particular physical strengths. Golf is a complex and difficult game, but not as complex as many people like to make it, nor quite as difficult when you build your technique around your best resources.

Finally, keep in mind that however much you think you know about this fascinating and frustrating game, there's always more to learn—and that however good you get at it, you can always get better.

Unfortunately, it took me a few years of mediocre playing and then one absolutely terrible season to relearn that last lesson. What's for sure is that I'll never let myself forget it again.

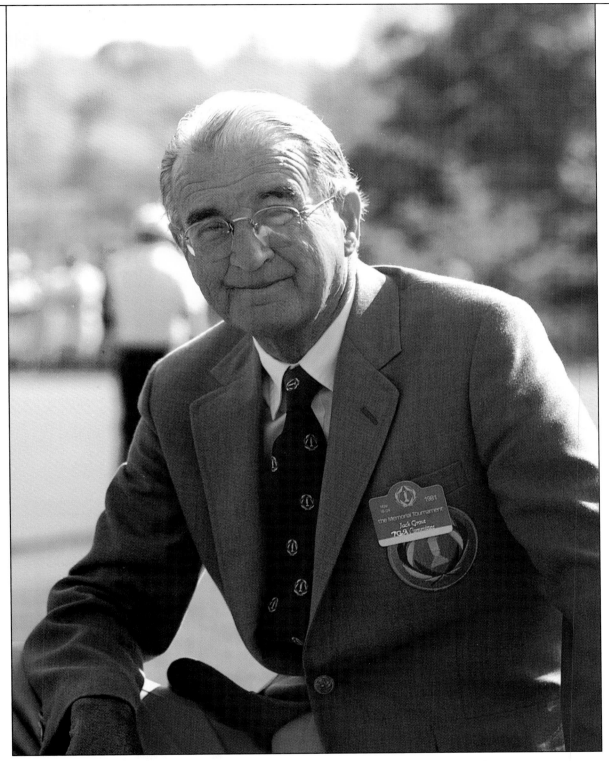

Jack Grout—a great friend, a great teacher, and the 1984 Captain of Muirfield Village Golf Club.